-EVERYDAY Ei-

Say This... Not That.

A Guide for Better Communication

Cynthia Howard RN, CNC, PhD

Copyright © 2017 Cynthia Howard RN, CNC, PhD

ISBN: 978-0-9907977-9-1

Cover design by Todd Siatkowsky, Special Forces Art Department

All rights reserved. No part of this book may be reproduced or transmitted in any form or by any means, electronic or mechanical, including photocopying, recording or by any information storage and retrieval system without written permission of the publisher, except for the inclusion of brief quotations in a review.

Printed in the United States of America.

TABLE OF CONTENTS

1. What This Book Is About 5
2. The Art of Conversation in a Digital Age 7
3. The Basics of Ei 13
4. E-Minders 18
   - Emotional Vocabulary 19
5. Self-Awareness: Emotional Fitness 22
6. Fatal Emotions 33
   - Drama at Work 37
   - Drama Self-check 39
   - 5 Destructive Divas 41
7. The C.A.R.E. Difference™: Model for Communication 45
   - Engage Your Body's Intelligence 47
8. You are the message 52
   - What Is a Brand? 52
   - Qualities of People with High Ei 55
   - Optimism 57
   - Manage Your "Mo" 58
   - Daily Review Journal 59
   - Communication Strategy 60
9. Toxic Conversations 62
   - The C.A.R.E Difference™ for Bullying 67
   - Sarcasm (Yeah, Right!) 70
   - Passive-Aggressiveness (Whatever!) 71
   - The C.A.R.E. Difference™ for Passive-Aggressiveness 74
   - Highly Sensitive? 80
   - Assertiveness 81

The C.A.R.E Difference™ for Assertiveness 85

10. Clichés and Idioms 87

11. Body language 92

12. Try Saying This Instead 95

13. Everyday Mindfulness 104

    Attention Reboot 109

14. Transforming Conflict 111

    The C.A.R.E. Difference™ with Conflict 115

    Active Listening 118

15. Empathy 121

16. Let's Continue This Conversation 126

    Develop Your Team's Communication Skills 130

Let's Keep in Touch! 131

Endnotes 132

EQi 2.0 Emotional Intelligence Assessment 134

C.A.R.E. Method™ at Your Organization 135

Ei Leadership Programs 136

About the Author 137

Other Books Written by Dr. Cynthia 138

1. WHAT THIS BOOK IS ABOUT

This is a guide to increase your awareness of your daily interactions and conversations. When you improve the value of your everyday conversations, you will improve your overall communication. Through conversations, you will build trust, deepen your connections with your coworkers, increase engagement, and enjoy greater work-life satisfaction.

Use this guide to reflect on what you truly want to communicate. What do you want someone to come away with after your exchange? Are you providing information and support, attempting to build trust, and offering an olive branch?

What Is Your Intention with Each Interaction?

As you become more aware, you can be more deliberate in your choice of phrases, gestures, and facial expressions. This increases the probability that the message you want to convey is what is received.

In the busyness of the day, it's easy to catch yourself giving robotic or cynical remarks that do little to connect authentically with our coworkers. This guide contains suggestions to increase the quality of your everyday interactions. More importantly, it is designed to encourage reflection and strengthen your emotional awareness and expression.

Emotional intelligence (Ei) has been shown to be a better predictor of success than clinical skills or training.

Ei is known to:

- Strengthen confidence
- Increase emotional flexibility
- Make it easier to adapt to what is happening
- Improve outcomes in the midst of challenges
- Improve work-life satisfaction

With better conversations in the workplace, you will have better results.

I look forward to your feedback. Enjoy the book.

"What if we don't change at all ... and something magical just happens?"

2. THE ART OF CONVERSATION IN A DIGITAL AGE

A conversation is two or more people talking together. Conversations include the exchange of words as well as nonverbal gestures like body language, facial expressions, and the tone and inflection in the speech. Conversations are more than the words that are spoken; they are an invitation into the world of the person speaking. Conversations *can* change the world.

Today, texting, emails, social media posts, and blogs are all ways that people communicate with each other, meaning face-to-face communication happens less often. I have heard people say they "prefer" texting to talking because it allows them time to respond and they avoid confrontations. To many, texting or chatting online is considered low-risk and can keep emotions from escalating.

Communicating via a digital device offers immediate feedback as people share images, emojis, and abbreviations, keeping content pithy and emotions superficial. The dialogue is simpler and less reflective. Reflection, as it takes place in a conversation, is an extension of listening, gives you the opportunity to make a deeper connection with the person talking, and increases your ability to learn. As conversations increasingly take place via a digital connection, some of the developmental skills that come from face-to-face conversations break down.

Research shows that when parents talk less frequently to their children and use technology to communicate, skills needed for friendship, work, and emotional connections are not developed.[1]

This shows up in recent college graduates coming into the workplace with anxieties and even phobias, including talking on the phone, having face-to-face interactions, and starting and ending conversations. Talking with someone face to face requires spontaneity, and this causes anxiety in some younger people who were raised via digital interactions by parents who text while talking without eye contact or focus.

Relying on technology for communication has changed most people's ability to be empathetic, read emotional cues, and confidently interact with others. Texting rather than talking decreases the ability to listen and respond in a way that keeps both parties in the conversation engaged.

The remedy for this digital disconnect? Have more face-to-face interactions and practice these skills.

An interesting research project found five days without devices increased a participant's ability to read emotions.[2] Five days was all it took! Do your own experiment and set up places and times that are device-free. Digital boundaries will support your efforts toward greater empathy and connection in the workplace.

Check out the following tips to unplug and quell FOMO (fear of missing out).

FOMO: Fear of Missing Out and What to Do About It

Anyone who has ever unplugged initially experiences this incredible *fear of missing out*. The way out of this fear is to expose yourself to times when you do not have the distraction of your device. You have to set up opportunities to interact with others to increase competency in conversation.

1. Set up technology-free zones at work. Leave the phone in a box at the door so you cannot check it. Researchers have found that having a phone on the table—even if it is face down—changes the dynamic of conversation.

2. Start the day with short stand-up, technology-free meetings. By encouraging eye contact and short conversations, your team can have the opportunity to connect with each other, build rapport, and increase their focus for the day.

3. Eye contact increases empathetic feelings. Research shows that social centers light up in the brain with even brief contact.[3] Empathy and self-awareness are linked; both are the root of emotional intelligence. Your ability to deal with people increases with face-to-face conversations.

4. Schedule time with coworkers or your direct reports rather than responding via email.

5. Establish a policy for yourself that you do not check email after a certain hour when you are at home.

6. Get an alarm clock and do not use your phone to wake you up.

7. When with your children, talk to them and resist using devices.
8. When with your coworkers, resist using devices and talk to each other.
9. Set up listening sessions for your direct reports. Once a month, schedule a time when they can present an idea and or a problem and you listen, ask questions only to clarify, and do not take over the dialogue.
10. Practice mindfulness. This is covered later in chapter thirteen.

Tips for Great Conversations

1. Ask open-ended questions. Here are a few ideas:
   a. What exciting thing are you working on today?
   b. What are you passionate about? What drives you?
   c. What are you grateful for today?
2. Getting people to talk about themselves is a powerful opening. Did you know that talking about yourself has the same positive impact as sex? The parts of the brain that are activated when talking about oneself are the same ones that light up with food, money, and sex, according to Harvard researchers Tamir and Mitchell.[4]
3. Practice active listening. I cover this in chapter fourteen, Transforming Conflict.
4. Conversations can carry an emotional charge. Are you aware of the impact of your message,

words, tone, gestures, and facial expressions? Tune into your message: are you triggering a fear response or does your message build trust?

5. Are you clear when you communicate? Conversations can be transactional or transformative. It is important to have both. What does the situation call for? What is your goal for the relationship you are building?

   a. Be aware of the meta-message with both of these and note the tone of voice, facial expressions, and words you're using, along with your body language. Conversations do not always end when the parties walk away; there is reflection (when one thinks about the meaning and the message). This can turn into rumination when the fear response is triggered during a conversation.

   b. Transactional conversations are informational and usually involve the transfer of facts or information.

   c. Transformational conversations can influence, persuade, and forge partnerships.

   d. Moving from a transactional to a transformational conversation requires deepening levels of trust. When you are sharing information, trust can be low and the information can still be transmitted. In a transactional conversation, one would tell someone something, ask pertinent questions, and keep to the point.

   e. When your goal is to influence or persuade, you want to build a partnership with your conversation. This requires building more trust and going beyond the sharing of information. Collaboration does not happen when one person is in a fear mode and your nervous system is fired up to protect you from some perceived threat.

This book offers ways to take your interactions from mediocre to meaningful. The next chapter is going to talk about emotional reactions and emotional intelligence.

3. THE BASICS OF Ei

Emotional intelligence (Ei) is a set of skills we can all develop. If you have a pulse and can choose if you like cream in your coffee, you have the ability to be emotionally aware and intelligent about how you use this awareness.

Think about Ei as the ability to know what you and others are feeling and then being able to manage those feelings for the best possible outcome.

These are four basic areas in Ei:

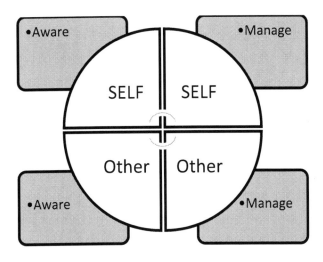

Emotions are hardwired into our nervous system, and whether we acknowledge the emotions or not, emotional reactions are triggered all day long. The only way you can be hijacked by your emotions is when you are unaware of them.

SAY THIS... NOT THAT.

The amazing brain and nervous system uses the fight, flight, or freeze reaction to react to any perceived threat. The emotional center of the brain is close by and tied into this instinctive reaction. The cortex, or thinking part of the brain, is the last to respond.

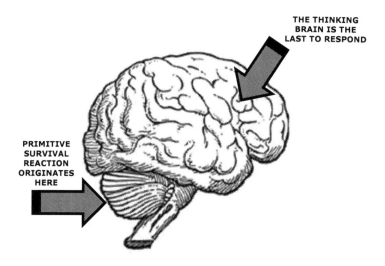

**You are hardwired:
first you feel, and then you think.**

This is why it's important to be tuned into what is going on inside of you so you can make adjustments as needed.

In a very large study with over 500,000 people, *only one third* were able to actually identify their feelings.[5] Many studies over several decades have found Ei to be the greatest predictor for success, so it makes sense to develop the skills that make up Ei.

I wrote this book and my others on resilience and Ei because it is time to make emotional intelligence as important as the clinical skills one possesses. I want this little guide to help you strengthen your Ei for better relationships and better results.

EQi 2.0:
Emotional Intelligence Assessment Tool

It is extremely powerful to have a baseline measure of Ei. I use the most scientifically validated tool, EQi 2.0. It measures sixteen different dimensions, giving you a snapshot of how you interact with your world.

After taking this assessment, you will know your strengths and have a plan to improve the performance of the dimensions you use less frequently. It is very accurate and immediately boosts confidence.

Here are the sixteen dimensions measured in the EQi 2.0:

1. **Self-regard**: Expressing your ideas and thoughts confidently and being comfortable in the process.

2. **Self-actualization**: Your ability to pursue meaningful goals and become the very best you can be.

3. **Emotional Self-awareness:** The foundation of emotional intelligence; when you know what is going on inside, you have the ability to act intentionally and in alignment with your goals.

4. **Emotional Expression**: Expressing your emotions in a direct way that is appropriate in intensity, thoughtful, respectful, and clear.

5. **Assertiveness:** Being respectful, intentional, and sensitive; setting limits and boundaries and stating your position clearly and evenly.

6. **Independence**: Working, thinking, and acting on your own and being a team member when needed.
7. **Relationships:** Your ability to work with people in order to get the job done.
8. **Empathy:** A set of skills, both emotional and behavioral, that allows one to connect with, understand, and relate to another in order to provide support.
9. **Social Responsibility**: Your ability to align with values of the greater good.
10. **Problem Solving**: Your ability to define the problem and find creative solutions; too often, problems are not well defined and initiatives fail.
11. **Reality Testing**: Increased awareness and insight into what you feel and how you see the world.
12. **Impulse Control**: Your ability to delay gratification for the benefit of your goals.
13. **Flexibility:** Your ability to adapt, shift, or adjust your behaviors, thoughts, and emotions to what is required of you in the moment.
14. **Stress Tolerance:** Resilience; your ability to bounce back from challenges without permanent damage.
15. **Optimism:** Your ability to hold positive expectations and remain hopeful and resilient, even in the face of challenge.
16. **Wellbeing**: Your overall sense of satisfaction with yourself and your life.

Which two dimensions are your strengths?
_____
_____
_____

Which two areas do you want to develop further?
_____
_____
_____

Check the resource in the back to take this assessment.

4. E-MINDERS

The positive power of your emotions:

1. Emotions convey information. Are you tuned in to your emotions so you can understand the best action you need to take in this situation?
2. If you ignore your emotions, they will show up at the worst possible time.
3. Emotions are not optional. The renowned neuroscientist, Damasio, has shown that you cannot make decisions without an intact emotional center.
4. People are motivated by emotion.
5. Emotions flow. When they get stuck, they cause moods or emotional storms.
6. Anger and rage are different. You can be angry without rage.
7. Just because you experience an emotion doesn't mean you have to express it at *that* moment with *that* person. It is likely its origin is from the past. Make a mental note and deal with it in the best time to achieve your ultimate goal.
8. Check in regularly. Reflect on why you acted in the way you did. Reflect on *both* positive and negative interactions.
9. Keep a journal.
10. Emotions are not good nor bad. When you can be neutral toward them, you can observe the impact

each has on you. Do they drain you, energize you, or flatten you? This is covered in the section on Emotional Fitness.

EMOTIONAL VOCABULARY

It is important to remember that emotions are neither good nor bad. Think of them like warning lights on your dashboard indicating a need to take some type of action.

Research shows that when you can name your feelings, you are more likely to control them. This ultimately cuts down on over- or under reactions.

Check out the following chart listing different emotions. Highlight those you would like to become more aware of.

SAY THIS... NOT THAT.

Notable Emotions

Angry	Determined	Fulfilled	Joyful
Affectionate	Delighted	Gregarious	Jealous
Adequate	Distant	Grateful	Lonely
Annoyed	Distraught	Glad	Loved
Anxious	Dubious	Guilty	Mad
Betrayed	Defeated	Happy	Miserable
Bitter	Eager	Hopeful	Overwhelmed
Bored	Energized	Honored	Overjoyed
Bodacious	Excited	Hardy	Panicked
Calm	Empty	Hopeless	Perplexed
Capable	Envious	Helpless	Peaceful
Challenged	Fatigued	Inspired	Pleased
Cheerful	Frustrated	Impressed	Proud
Confused	Foolish	Intimidated	Relieved
Content	Friendly	Irritated	Refreshed
Relaxed	Satisfied	Unsettled	
Safe	Threatened	Vulnerable	
Sad	Trapped	Ashamed	

DR. CYNTHIA HOWARD

**You will make mistakes.
You will experience others'
mistakes. Your Ei will help
you get beyond that
and grow.**

5. SELF-AWARENESS: EMOTIONAL FITNESS

Most people go through their day locked into a habitual pattern of reacting. It is only when you begin to question your reactions and emotions that you begin to understand what you are feeling and why.

Take a moment and reflect on the history of your emotional patterns. In reflecting you have the opportunity to breakthrough any patterns that no longer work for you.

The more aware you are of what is going on within you, the more you can manage what is happening around you.

The exercise on the next page helps you clarify your patterns. This is a great introduction to your emotions. These exercises build self-awareness, a hallmark of a successful leader.

To help you tune in and become more aware of your emotional experiences, evaluate the following questions:

ANGER · HAPPINESS · ANXIETY · FEAR · SADNESS

1. Looking at the feelings above. What feeling is usually most intense for you using a 1-10 scale?

    0 ——————————— 10

    Feeling: _____

2. What feeling is most frequent on a 1-10 scale?

   0 ——————————————— 10

   Feeling: _____

3. What is the typical outcome as a result of this feeling? Does it impact your relationships, job, energy levels, or motivation?

   _____

   _____

   _____

Next, we will look at each emotion individually. Take the time to reflect on these questions and journal your answers.

ANGER

How do you know you are angry? What do you feel in your body?

_____

_____

_____

What happens as a result of experiencing anger?

_____

_____

_____

How does it affect other people?

_____

_____

How does it interfere with your goals?

_____

_____

_____

How would you prefer to experience anger?

_____

_____

_____

Who or what flips your anger switch on?

_____

_____

_____

_____

Anger is an important emotion. I want you to get to know your anger. When ignored, anger turns to rage, resentment, heart disease, and worse, it shuts down your ability to be happy and enjoy your life.

Remember, emotions are neither good nor bad. They are designed to inform you.

What Anger Is Telling You

Remembering that all emotions are designed to flow and inform, know that anger alerts you to set boundaries and facilitate change. That could be simply putting your hand up and saying, "Stop," when someone is attempting to force you to do something you do not want to do or talking at you and disrespecting your space.

Anger is a universal emotion that has a variety of styles of expression across different cultures, families, and genders. Women are more than likely taught to hold it in, while men are taught to express it. Some people see anger as a masculine emotion.

Most people deny their anger for a variety of reasons. When this happens, you can count on it showing up at the worst possible time. Like all emotions, anger is an internal signal to take some sort of action.

Denying your anger can increase the use of sarcasm, passive-aggressive behaviors, and other mixed signals, decreasing your ability to communicate clearly. The reflection exercise on the previous page will help you be aware of when anger shows up and its impact on you and the people around you.

Heart-focused breathing will be introduced in chapter seven in the section, *Your Body's Intelligence*. This technique, when practiced regularly, will help you tame your anger.

HAPPINESS

How do you know you are happy? What do you feel in your body?

_____

_____

_____

What happens as a result of experiencing happiness?

_____

_____

SAY THIS... NOT THAT.

How does it enhance your goal?

_____

_____

_____

What would it take to experience more happiness?

_____

_____

_____

What experiences flip your happiness switch on?

_____

_____

_____

Happiness is an individual experience. Thousands of years ago, Aristotle recognized that more than anything, people sought happiness. People seek happiness for its own sake. It can be an experience that defies words.

Defining happiness is difficult, and people often start out by saying what happiness is not. It is not having all the money or time in the world. It is doing something meaningful. It is not feeling good all the time nor is it a destination. It is fleeting, elusive, and takes time. Trying too hard definitely gets in the way of happiness.

Happiness is on a continuum and includes feeling cheerful, satisfied, content, as well as optimistic. It is personal.

Boredom is a barrier to happiness. And boredom is telling you to stretch yourself, grow, and learn something new. Happiness is best achieved in the act of reaching for a goal and doing something you did not think you could do.

Be sure to reflect on the questions and journal your answers. The more you cultivate happiness, the less likely you will get stuck in an emotional storm.

ANXIETY

How do you know you are anxious? What do you feel in your body?

_____

_____

_____

What happens as a result of experiencing anxiety?

_____

_____

_____

How does it interfere with your goal?

_____

_____

_____

What would you like to experience instead?

_____

_____

_____

Who or what flips your anxiety switch on?

SAY THIS... NOT THAT.

_____

_____

_____

Fear, when chronic and generalized, becomes anxiety. Anxiety arises from thoughts. It can catch you in an endless thought loop. Did I sign off on that contract? Did I forget something? What if *xyz* happens—what then? And on and on and on. Many people I talk to experience this type of endless questioning at the end of the day.

What Anxiety Is Telling You

Anxiety, when not chronic, can serve as a messenger to help you clarify a situation in your life and take action.

When anxiety becomes chronic, it can be the body's way of avoiding something. Chronic anxiety shrinks your world in the effort to avoid feeling the anxiety. Phobias become a way of coping with the anxiety.

Anxiety, as part of the fear emotion, wants you to take some sort of action. Much of the anxiety people experience results from constant distractions and not being able to remember what they've done. Use your phone to create lists or download one of the many apps that will help you stay organized and focused.

Be sure to reflect on the questions and journal your answers.

FEAR

How do you know you are fearful? What do you feel in your body?

_____

_____

_____

What happens as a result of experiencing fear?

_____

_____

_____

How does it interfere with your goal?

_____

_____

_____

What would you like to experience instead?

_____

_____

_____

Who or what flips your fear switch on?

_____

_____

_____

Fear is an emotion that comes from the amygdala, the alarm system in your nervous system hardwired to protect us from danger. It is instinctive, and the reaction happens instantaneously. The amygdala sends the trigger to the hypothalamus, which then creates the physiological patterns for that fear. Your heartrate can go up, and you might feel a lump in your throat, tension in your neck, numbness in your hands, and any number of other physical reactions.

Fear triggers the fight-or-flight response in the stress reaction. Your amygdala is the storehouse of all your fear experiences (even those you forget) and responds immediately when it senses an experience similar to what has been stored. Most of the time, people are not aware of the origin of their fear and may not be consciously aware of their reaction.

Confronting your fears helps you overcome the instinctive pull of this primitive reaction. Fears are usually specific to a person, place, or situation and arise from feelings.

Use the heart-focused breathing exercise included in this book to activate resilience. This lessens the fear reaction. Be sure to reflect on the questions and journal.

SADNESS

How do you know you are sad? What do you feel in your body?

_____
_____
_____

What happens as a result of experiencing sadness?

_____
_____

How does it interfere with your goal?

_____

_____

_____

What would you like to experience instead?

_____

_____

_____

Who or what flips your sadness switch on?

_____

_____

_____

Sadness is not the same as depression, although it is frequently associated with it. Depression is a more complex experience. There are the clinical definitions of depression—bipolar disorder, postpartum depression, dysthymia, mild depression, atypical depression, and major depression.

Sadness is not the same as grief. Grief shows up in response to losses that are irretrievable. Grief can happen as a result of a physical death or the death of a dream, an opportunity, a period in your life, part of your body—any loss that is gone forever. There are stages of grief, and—as with all emotions—it is best to move through grief present and mindful to what you are experiencing.

I highly recommend having help in moving through grief because one loss will trigger other losses you have experienced, and it quickly can feel overwhelming.

What Sadness Is Telling You

Sadness, with its heaviness, the desire to withdraw, and the need to cry, is a cue you need time to reflect, review your life, and let go of things that are not working. Sadness gives you a window into what you value. This helps you understand yourself better. When you can acknowledge your own sadness, increases your ability to demonstrate empathy. By acknowledging sadness and moving through it, you develop courage and the ability to do other difficult things. Sadness is like other emotions and is designed to flow. Acknowledge it, and remind yourself, "This too shall pass."

When sadness is not acknowledged and is ignored, you can move into despair, which is a mood and lacks the natural flow built into sadness. Crying can often provide the relief needed to let go, and, with the release of tension, you can relax and begin to restore yourself. You have heard the sayings, "I just need a good cry," or, "Have a good cry, and you will feel better." This wisdom speaks to the cleansing and refreshing nature of moving through sadness.

Get to know how sadness shows up for you; reflect on the questions and journal your answers.

6. FATAL EMOTIONS

We have all received some type of disappointing news. Your promotion did not come through, the raise wasn't what you expected, you lost the bid for the job, you did not get accepted into your program—the list can go on.

Disappointment is part of living life. When you do not manage those disappointments and you become discouraged, that can be fatal. Discouragement that goes unchecked destroys self-image, confidence, and expectations for the future.

Discouragement

The dictionary definition of discouragement is "the act of making something less likely to happen." When discouragement is allowed to grow into a mood, motivation and momentum are eroded.

The erosion can be subtle. The discouragement shifts to a feeling that "things will never work out." You may try harder only to experience more disappointment, or you may give up altogether. Either way, discouragement kills drive.

This is why self-awareness is so important. You have to be able to identify your feelings and then take the right action to shift them.

Go from Discouraged to Determined

1. **Name it:** Whenever you feel disappointment, identify it and take action.

2. **Reframe it**: Identify three things that are going well for you.

3. **Claim it**: Engage the optimist in you and recognize that it is not permanent and things will change. Denial is what makes this emotion fatal, capable of destroying your mojo.

4. **Talk about it:** (Or, write in your journal.) Find a safe person who will simply listen. At this point, talking it out helps release the heavy emotion. You can find solutions later.

5. **Help someone else**: The tendency with discouragement is to narrow your focus and think only of your problems. Get out of yourself and reach out to someone in need.

6. **Move on**: Let it go and focus on your big vision.

In addition to these steps, do something every day to manage the stressful feelings that come up. We have a module in the Work SMART Club on proven five-minute strategies you can use in the moment to interrupt the fight-or-flight reaction. The more you practice these, the stronger your resilience.

Let's talk about the *most* fatal emotion, one that only happens to everyone else—denial.

Denial

It is a defense mechanism we *all* use to protect ourselves from some perceived threat. Maybe there was bad news and you instinctively minimize it to get through the emergency. This temporary use of denial is helpful.

Denial becomes fatal when you use it to avoid dealing with situations that require action. Drinking too much, avoiding dealing with financial strain, avoiding your bullying coworker, or signs your teenager is using drugs, ignoring the fact you are using food to compensate for your disappointments—these are all examples of denial that is fatal.

You can deny your own behavior or that of others. Denying your own behavior shows up in chronic blaming. If you persistently accuse others of doing something wrong, chances are the problem lies with you.

Here is an example. A client came to me distressed and ready to quit her job because her boss was blaming her for misplacing reports in the office. He was disorganized and never put anything away, so piles would grow on his desk. He would call her and accuse her of taking the document and not returning it. She did not want to talk to him about it and decided to avoid any conflict.

It is helpful to realize that in any interaction, both people are responsible for the outcome. Are you contributing to a situation by trying to avoid it?

When you avoid taking any action, you are denying your responsibility in the situation. If you feel like a victim and complain, "Things always happen to me," chances are you are using denial to avoid taking action.

Denial allows problematic situations and health risks to continue, ultimately creating more serious issues. If you have been exposed to traumatic events or are reaching exhaustion and you continue to push yourself, the body's ability to adapt reaches its limit and you can hit the wall. It is important to address the signs of burnout long before you crash.

It is important to address issues with your staff and followers before they become a much bigger issue. When denial is allowed to operate within a culture, you turn off creativity and initiative. Motivation comes from the recognition one can make a difference. In a culture steeped in denial, people essentially go to sleep.

What beliefs keep you from seeing problems as they show up?

Being realistic and facing the challenge is a characteristic of a high Ei leader.

The value of denial is as a short-term defense mechanism.

Suggestions to Go Beyond Denial

1. Open up to feedback. Before you shut out what someone tells you, consider this: is there any truth to what they are saying?

2. Get in touch with your fears. Does change threaten you? Afraid to succeed? What are your fears?

3. Talk to someone—counselor or coach. Your friends or family are not going to move you ahead. Talk with a professional.

4. Evaluate your life to date. Is it working out the way you expected or has it fallen short? If so, in what way? Be objective. Have your beliefs held you back? What are they?

5. Journal every day. Use the Daily Review to reflect on what is working and what isn't. Keep this for a year, and you will have a timeline review you can use to evaluate patterns of success, avoidance, progress, or resistance.

DRAMA AT WORK

Drama is draining. Do you agree?

This is what most people complain about—the "politics" of the workplace: gossip, popularity contests, excessive competition, bullying, and the battle to be heard and understood drain energy faster than anything else. Work days are longer and harder with this toxic behavior contributing to low productivity and low morale.

The cost of low productivity to the organization is in the billions with staff turnover, error, risk, and poor patient outcomes. The defensive patterns of drama derail teamwork, collaboration, and destroy productivity.

There are three "drama" conversations that take place.[6] Without self-awareness, this conversation becomes a vicious cycle and you end up switching roles, going from victim to persecutor. The outcome of these conversations is to perpetuate powerlessness and avoid accountability.

These patterns are defense mechanisms that allow each person to stay stuck or in the status quo. Most of the time, these patterns are unconscious; they come from a set of beliefs (with emotional cues) that undermine one's self-confidence and self-image. The way out is self-awareness and development of assertiveness, emotional expression, and other skills within emotional intelligence. I will share a model of communication that interrupts this process.

"Poor Me"

Feeling hopeless, helpless conversation comes from the "Victim" blocking decisions and interfering with problem solving and progress moving forward.

This conversation needs a "Rescuer" to jump in to save the day in order to keep the cycle going.

"I Will Save the Day"

The "Rescuer" helps even when they do not want to and ends up feeling resentful. The person feels guilty if they do not help and experiences positive self-worth by helping others. This cycle enables failure rather than accountability and empowerment where people are a part of the solution.

"It's Your Fault"

This cycle of destructive communication starts with the blaming, shaming, and criticism from a "Persecutor." In spite of the confrontational tone of this conversation, this person is coming from a powerless position, as are the other two.

The motivation behind these three roles is to avoid expressing needs and or wishes directly. By relying on these defenses, you focus on protecting your own needs (versus the needs of the group or the greater good). This can happen when the primitive survival instinct of the fight-or-flight reaction gets triggered; it is easy to lose perspective and react to fears that come up.

As you increase resilience and strengthen emotional intelligence, you avoid these destructive patterns.

Before I share the four-step model of effective communication, take the Drama Self-check.

DRAMA SELF-CHECK

Read through the questions. Answer using a 1 to 10 scale with 10 being "All the time," and 1 being "Rarely." Keep in mind, just about everyone does some of this some of the time.

Your goal is to increase your awareness of your communication style—not to be perfect. It's important to understand your underlying feelings, like powerlessness or anger, that may be underneath these behaviors.

SAY THIS... NOT THAT.

1 2 3 4 5 6 7 8 9 10
Rarely   All the Time

1. Do you provide unsolicited advice?
2. Do you jump to help even when not asked?
3. Do you compromise to avoid conflict and feel resentful or withdraw from the process?
4. Do you use intimidation to get your way?
5. Are you impatient when things do not go your way?
6. Do you take feedback as a personal attack?
7. Do you feel like you are the only one committed to the project and get frustrated with others?
8. Do you withhold your feelings or opinions because you feel like they won't matter?

Your Score: _____

The higher your score, the greater the chance you are engaging in the drama roles of victim, rescuer, or persecutor. What stood out to you as you went through the questions?

What will you differently?

_____
_____
_____

Next, check out the 5 Destructive Divas...

5 DESTRUCTIVE DIVAS

Have you ever called in "sick" (of your coworkers)?

In this section, I have laid out five different roles people play at work that disrupt productivity and morale.

Do you work with any of them? Have you been like any of them? If so, don't beat yourself up! What matters now is that you begin to identify any behaviors that may be sabotaging your success.

1. Drama Diva

Using words like *everything, always, never*, and *making mountains out of molehills*, this diva is determined to be noticed and get attention. Emotions really are our GPS (guidance for professional success); however, Drama Divas use their emotions like the siren on emergency vehicles, lights flashing and alarms blasting. You cannot miss hearing or seeing this person. The problem with this diva is even if the issue is relevant, this person is often discounted because the drama overrides the ability to tune in and track with this person.

2. Detached Diva

This individual is distant and aloof and does not interact or join in any unit activities. There could be a hidden layer of resentment or fear of rejection setting up a barrier to getting to know anyone. The detachment can be interpreted by others as indifference, creating gossip or judgement toward that person. This is a problem because when help is needed, this person is so used to working alone that they do not notice when someone needs help. Their standoffishness also keeps others from asking them for help. This breaks up the cohesiveness of the team.

3. No-Way Diva

This individual says "no" or complains about everything before they even know what it is. This individual makes it tough to ask for help because you know they will say "no." This person finds ways to get out of doing work and is happy to let other people do the jobs they do not want to do. They get away with it because no one wants to confront them. This diva will intimidate their coworkers when necessary.

4. BFF Diva

This diva is friendly to a fault—interested in hearing all about your weekend, plans for vacation, and even what you are making for dinner, but not interested in doing any work. While friendly, this diva does not like to be told they are slacking and will claim they are building team spirit and keeping the morale up.

5. Super Diva

This diva is the Superhero of the unit, wanting to be all things to all people. Not able to say "no," this individual takes on tasks and assignments wanting to do everything themselves. This martyrdom usually comes with some resentment and feeling like they are better than everyone else. This diva has issues with control and may feel like they have to prove something to others. It creates resentment and tension in the team as others feel like they need to compete. This person is also more likely to burn out.

Are you a Diva? Shift to Delightful

1. Learn to laugh at yourself and recognize we are all growing, learning, and developing personally and professionally.
2. Spend some quiet time and reflect on what you need. How do you feel most heard and validated? Set up a plan to get it.
3. Before you express yourself verbally, write it out. This will diffuse any intense emotions and help you express yourself more rationally.
4. Recognize that working together as part of a team is what makes work more enjoyable and less stressful. Be a part of the solution.
5. Breathe deeply for five seconds before you say anything.
6. Recognize that your behavior has an impact on everyone in your department. Check in with yourself and ask the question, "Would I want to work with someone like me?"

SAY THIS... NOT THAT.

What Team Members Can Do to Help the Diva Shift

1. Provide supportive feedback to the Divas, recognizing there could be something going on that is creating this behavior.
2. Speak directly to the person rather than talking about the person or the behavior behind their back.
3. Let them know they are a valuable part of the team and their help is needed in order to meet the department's goals.
4. Work together to establish expectations for teamwork and attitude on your unit. Keep it positive and related to professional growth. Post this in your break room and have everyone sign it.

The motivation for these behaviors and that of the drama triangle come from unconscious needs or desires. Here is where the assessment tools like the Myers Briggs, EQi 2.0, and or the TKI: Conflict Instrument can spotlight one's personal preferences and open up the group to a much deeper understanding of each other.

Developing a good team is not just the role of management. In the next section, I will present a model to help you communicate more authentically with coworkers and your staff.

7. THE C.A.R.E. DIFFERENCE™: MODEL FOR COMMUNICATION

I first presented this model of C.A.R.E. in my book, *Resilience: Your Super Power*.[7] Care is one of the hardest things for healthcare professionals to balance, and it is the common denominator in resilience and emotional intelligence.

The ability to take care of yourself is what those who regularly demonstrate resilience and Ei, have in common. I decided to use this acronym as the model for better communication and performance. This model will help you move from the struggle of the three drama conversations to effective communication.

The survival instinct in the fight-or-flight reaction shuts down access to your internal resources that provide perspective, empathy, creativity, and meaning. Without access to these, it doesn't take long to burn out. Worse, when someone burns out, they often do not realize it until they have lost opportunities and relationships and hopelessness and cynicism replaces vision and confidence.

This model of C.A.R.E. will focus on four dimensions to break the cycle of knee-jerk reactions in your communication. The C.A.R.E. model recognizes that to engage Ei every day, you have to be aware of your interactions, your internal dialogue, and, the resources available.

When operating in the survival mode of the stress reaction, it is easy to overlook your and others' feelings and what is happening in the environment.

Here is the four-step process:

C: Connect

Question for you: What am I feeling?

Move out of the struggle with this person and think about how you can make a connection with them. To do that, first connect within and identify your feelings.

A: Awareness

Question for you: How will I handle my feelings?

Identify your hot buttons, needs, desires, and preferences for work. Take assessments to get to know yourself. Be aware of what is going on within you, especially during your interactions. This prevents blaming or shaming the other person.

R: Resilience

Question for you: What perspective will create understanding?

Conflict, drama, and other difficult situations trigger emotions and the fight-or-flight response. This primitive survival instinct puts you in a weak position versus operating from your strengths.

Practice resilient building strategies every day that will interrupt the fight-or-flight reaction. Your goal is to get to a place of neutral, to engage in active listening and the desire to solve a problem versus giving up, attacking, or rescuing. Getting to neutral is explained in the next section, *Engage Your Body's Intelligence.*

E: Empower

Question for you: How can I resolve this?

This step is designed to empower you and the other person to find a solution and build accountability. Resist rescuing that person and doing things for them. Are there resources needed to take care of the problem and build a solution?

Use C.A.R.E. to remind yourself to balance care for others with yourself and use the four-step process for a healthy interaction.

Before I move on to another section, I want to elaborate on the "Rescuer" pattern of behavior. This is one role that people struggle with. After all, they "only want to make things better."

The key to caring as a healthcare professional without burning out or coming down with "compassion fatigue" is to recognize *you* also have needs, just like everyone else. I talk about over-care in the section on empathy.

ENGAGE YOUR BODY'S INTELLIGENCE

Have stress, overwhelm, fatigue, and irritability become the new normal at your workplace? Many people do not recognize they are in a chronic stress mode with cortisol surging through their body, heartrate up, blood pressure up, breathing shallower, and perspective narrowed due to the survival focus of the fight-of-flight reaction.

I want to share a simple yet powerful technique to unhook from this stress reaction. Before I do, I want to talk about why this is so important to move out of overdrive into neutral.

Chronic unchecked stress leads to disease. The immune system becomes suppressed, increasing the opportunity for colds, flu, auto-immune conditions, and even cancers to take over the body's ability to fight back. Heart disease is a greater risk for those who live with chronic stress.

Unchecked stress makes you susceptible to distraction, greater irritability, anxiety, and excessive rumination. It doesn't take long before everything becomes catastrophic and your mind gets stuck in an endless loop of worst case scenarios.

What happens to your relationships at work and at home when you are stressed out? Going through the day in overdrive derails your best effort at applying emotional intelligence; survival needs trump resilient thinking and calm interactions. You feel first and think later.

You may end up speaking in short, terse commands and becoming more forgetful and much more irritable, seeing your team as "stupid," not even aware of how you look to others. Interrupt this vicious cycle with a regular practice of heart-focused breathing.

This is just one of the techniques in the Heartmath®[8] System of stress management.

I have been a Heartmath® provider for many years, and I've used these techniques with my clients. It is just one of the power tools in my toolkit to activate resilience.

To help you see what this will do for you, imagine yourself in your car, stopped at a red light. It is hot outside, and while in drive, the RPMs are revved up and you can feel the vibration. Now, put the car into neutral and notice what happens to the RPMs: they drop and the sound of the car gets much quieter. You can feel the car's vibration slow down. This is what happens when you learn to put *you* into neutral using this technique.

With regular practice, you will activate resilience, decrease your stress set point, manage the endless thought loops of disaster, and engage creativity and empathy. You will increase your focus and concentration, even during stressful times.

Ready?

Heart-Focused Breathing

You are breathing already; breathe more intentionally. Chronic stress decreases the urge to deep breathe, which is a natural antidote to the tension experienced in chronic stress.

First, bring your attention to the area around your heart. Imagine your breath going in and around your heart. Breathe in and out, on a count of four. Inhale on a count of four. Hold it on a count of four, then exhale on a count of four. Repeat.

Now, bring up a feeling of gratitude or appreciation. Intensify this feeling. Breathe in gratitude and exhale your frustration, using the four-count breathing. Repeat. Continue to breathe normally, expanding the feeling of gratitude or appreciation.

Did you know that the heart has its own intelligence network? While the nervous system has a big job in controlling the fight-or-flight response, it is the heart and the thousands of chemicals that are sent *up* to the brain that bring the body and the brain into balance.

The feelings of gratitude and appreciation are the language of the heart and act to harmonize the body and the brain. This was discovered after decades of research by the Institute of Heartmath, along with many others.

As you slow down your heartrate and engage the language of the heart with gratitude and appreciation, you shift out of survival mode. Think about a time when you were in flow, when time passed without notice, and even though you may have been working hard, you felt good. With regular practice of this routine, you train your nervous system to engage this flow state more regularly.

Tips to Make This Work for You

1. Set timers on your phone for two-hour intervals to remind yourself to engage in this twenty-second practice.
2. Breathe in and out, imagining the area around your heart, using the four count. Repeat four times.
3. Breathe in gratitude or appreciation using this four count. Exhale frustration (or the distracting emotion).

4. Breathe normally and allow the feeling of gratitude or appreciation to grow and expand beyond you.
5. Practice this for fifteen to twenty seconds. Increase to sixty seconds.
6. When thoughts come into your mind, let them drift out and bring your focus back to your breath.

With regular practice, you will be more mindful and present. Use this before and during any difficult conversation. With regular practice, it becomes easier and you build your "resilience muscle."

When do five rights make it *all* right?

Anybody can become angry—that is easy,
but to be angry with the right person and
to the right degree and at the right time and
for the right purpose, and in the right way—
that is not within everybody's power and is not easy.

—Aristotle, born 384 BC

8. YOU ARE THE MESSAGE

As leaders, it is paramount that you set the tone for your department or organization. Without a strong message, informal leaders pop up and derail your message, and it becomes an uphill battle to manage and lead.

If you are not in an official leadership role, this section is just as important for your future advancement.

You are the message. This section introduces "branding" to help you understand that how people perceive you is as important as who you believe you are. You have the responsibility to control the message and send clear, strong signals to your followers.

WHAT IS A BRAND?

Branding has grown in meaning from the early days of branding cattle, used to identify the ranch it came from, to the trademark of a product. Today, brand includes the perception people have about the product.

It includes the logo, jingle, colors, and other graphics. More importantly, it is the expectation people have for that product. Brand is what people perceive about the product. *Coca-Cola*, one of the most well-known and persuasive brands, sells happiness, not caramel-colored soda. This perception crosses generational and cultural differences. People naturally associate fun-loving, happy activities with *Coca-Cola*.

What is your brand? How do people perceive you, and what are the expectations people have of you?

> **Your brand represents the value you bring to the people you serve.**

Brand includes the responsibility (ownership) of what you say and do, along with the accountability for daily choices. Every day, your followers have an expectation, a standard for what you deliver—this is your brand.

Your brand is what others say you are, by way of your actions, words, attitude, dress, and value system. This is why consistent performance is critical as a leader.

Strengthening your Ei will build self-awareness so you can be deliberate and intentional with your brand. As you do this, it becomes easier to get this consistent performance from others.

Make sense so far? Jot down any questions as you go through this guide and get the clarification to make this system work for you.

> **Why do you want to invest the time into developing your brand?**

1. The consistent expression of who you are and what you represent will increase trust with your followers.
2. Increase opportunities. As you own your brand, other leaders may see something in you they want on their team. Brand can be the magnetic draw for better opportunities.

SAY THIS... NOT THAT.

3. Increase your confidence. As you own and act on your strengths, you will develop competencies and respect yourself more. This is an authentic representation of you as a leader.
4. Unless you intentionally develop your brand, you are sending out messages about who you are that may actually hurt you.

Suggestions

1. Write a weekly blog. This will help you formulate your values and express them to your team. If humor is one of your strengths and what you would like to build in your team, share a funny anecdote weekly; ask others to send a short story back. You can even open your meetings with a funny story or a joke; this is powerful when you put it in the context of what you are presenting.

   What values are important to you? What is the priority? Do your daily choices reflect this?

2. Dress the way you want people to perceive you. Do you need a wardrobe makeover?
3. It is easy to mimic your mentor or someone you admire; however, it never works out the way you think. Pinpoint the characteristic you admire and own it in yourself. Take some "me" time and get to know yourself. Express your best characteristics.
4. Take the EQi 2.0 assessment listed in the back of this book. It will help you identify your strengths and build confidence.

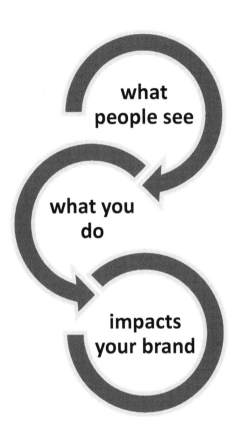

QUALITIES OF PEOPLE WITH HIGH EI

Curious

Ask questions, get to know what makes people who they are; relates to empathy.

Don't Take Things Personally

Check out the book, *The 4 Agreements* by Ruiz.[9]

Embrace Change
FLOW means you seek challenges.

Self-aware
Know your strengths and weaknesses, and have a plan in place to deal with both.

Emotional Vocabulary
When you can name your feelings, you gain control over them.

Set Boundaries
Able to say yes or no, depending on what is best for the desired outcome.

Do Not Take Responsibility for Others
You are responsible for the outcomes, not what everyone else does.

Take Care of Themselves
Make daily choices to support your best self (sleep, food, positive thoughts, etc.).

Balance Perfection with High Performance
Deal with fears of failure without getting bogged down with nagging worries about being perfect.

Manage Conflict and Difficult People
It is easy to "let things work out on their own;" however, this is often abdication of your responsibility. Deal with the conflict and set the tone for your department.

Grateful

Every day, write down three things you are grateful for; make this a ritual, and you will find yourself enjoying your day more.

Appreciate Other People

Be generous with your appreciation; let people know that who they are and what they do means a lot to you.

OPTIMISM

This is a skill that comes naturally to some and, for others, is a skill you can develop. The daily grind of getting things done can squeeze an optimistic attitude. Optimism fuels Ei and resilience and protects you from the fatal emotions we just talked about.

The first image many have of "optimism" is Pollyanna—a consistently positive person who never sees a challenge. This is a limited, flat view of optimism.

Positive thinking is just the first part of optimism; you also have to be realistic and understand the challenges to be prepared.

I have heard people say that one must be "realistically optimistic." This implies that being positive will get you in trouble. This is the same as saying you don't want to give "false hope."

Optimism is a blend of holding a vision that things will work out while being realistic about what is in front of you. It requires you be confident in your strengths, aware of your weaknesses, and *capable of focusing on what needs to be done.*

SAY THIS... NOT THAT.

An optimistic attitude has three parts. Optimists see the situation as temporary and random as opposed to permanent and personal. Pessimists would say, "I always get left out . . ." Optimists say, "My chances are good to get picked next time . . ." And third, an optimistic attitude recognizes (and expects) success *will* happen at some point.

Unchecked stress destroys optimism because of the survival nature of the stress reaction. The nervous system is hardwired to focus on problems due to its primitive survival instinct.

Be sure to set up daily strategies to deal with overwhelm and frustration and protect your attitude!

Cultivate optimism in yourself and others.

HAPPY

MANAGE YOUR "MO"

John Maxwell talks about the "Law of Big Mo," referring to momentum. I am referring to your motivation. This can easily get squashed in the daily grind and long to-do list. Emotional intelligence is the ability to recognize your needs and then do something about them.

Your performance depends on you taking care of yourself. This may require you to learn new skills, hire a coach to help you with your mindset, or start exercising to build stamina. Adopt an attitude of continual learning, and you will manage your "mo."

Which people, places, or situations dampen your motivation?

_____

_____

_____

What increases your motivation?

_____

_____

_____

The next tip will help you focus.

DAILY REVIEW JOURNAL

At the end of every day, spend five to fifteen minutes reflecting on the following questions:

1. What worked?
2. What didn't work?
3. What's next?

On Fridays, do a review of the week. At the end of the month, review the month.

Set a timer on your phone to remind you it is time to do the review. Eventually, it will become a habit. Use the timer to keep this review brief (five to fifteen minutes). The power of this review is in the daily application. It doesn't help to binge and review for an hour once a week.

This will help you reflect on conversations, interactions, priorities, and outcomes. It will increase your self-awareness.

You can use a computer app or write this out in a notebook.

COMMUNICATION STRATEGY

I wanted to talk briefly about the broader meaning of communication. Conversations are part of a communication strategy that includes all forms of messaging, those conveyed individually and at the departmental or organizational level.

Organizational communication includes conveying the mission, vision, and other conceptual ideas. It includes inspiring the team to align with the overall mission and vision of the organization. Messages need to include the emotional hook, a sense of urgency, and the reason why aligning with this overall organization is important.

Leaders need to establish trust with staff and learn how to convey these ideas so they will engage. Too often, the message conveyed is not the message received because of the meta-message that goes along with it. This could include gossip about the idea and misinformation.

Are you timely and clear in the delivery of the message?

It is important to share data and support the call to action when prompting certain expected behaviors.

Is the data compelling, understandable, and relevant?

In healthcare, it is necessary to communicate across the continuum of care. Research shows that as many as one fourth of readmissions could be avoided with better communication. Having a strategy to communicate that includes digital devices *and* face-to-face communication is important to build rapport among the professionals in various disciplines and across departments.

Are professionals establishing trust with each other through appreciation within the departments and across the continuum?

What makes a strategy effective is how the individuals in the organization convey their message. This is what makes Ei and communication skills at the top of the list for professional development.

The next chapter talks about the destructive forces that break down even the best laid communication strategy.

9. TOXIC CONVERSATIONS

Every workplace has its share of hassles, conflict, and turbulence. Toxic workplaces make this seem normal and engage in destructive measures that keep it going.

Toxic environments cannot be changed alone. This cultural challenge requires strong leadership, a positive vision, and clearly communicated expectations for behavior.

If you are in a toxic environment, you may want to plan an exit strategy. If you do stay, have a plan to protect yourself from the highly reactive interactions that frequently take place. Toxic workplaces can destroy self-esteem and confidence and weaken your desire to operate at your best.

In this chapter, I will be addressing bullying, passive-aggressiveness, and more, offering tips on handling these situations. Regardless of what someone does or says, you are one hundred percent accountable for your response. This chapter gives you a healthy approach to transform toxic into tolerable.

Seven Signs of a Toxic Workplace

1. Bullying is accepted
2. Unfair workload
3. Gossip predominates
4. Deadlines missed, productivity suffers

5. Use of fear or intimidation to coerce employees
6. Staff or managers covering for each other rather than openly addressing performance issues
7. Status quo mindset

As you think about where you work, how would you rate your workplace? Use the 1–10 scale, with 10 being very toxic. Write down a toxic behavior you have experienced.

      1 2 3 4 5 6 7 8 9 10

_____

_____

_____

_____

_____

Now, let's look at the characteristics of a healthy workplace.

A healthy workforce is productive.

Check out this list describing a healthy workplace. What else would you add to the list?

Ten Signs of a Healthy Workplace

1. Emphasis on positive communication
2. Commitment to excellence, high standards
3. Sense of humor
4. Trust throughout the organization
5. Open communication
6. Respect and civility for each other

SAY THIS... NOT THAT.

7. Collaboration
8. Recognition of the link between wellbeing and performance
9. Balance in work, play, and family
10. Decisive and flexible leadership
11. _____
12. _____

Bullying

Bullying is a systematic process by one person or multiple people who seek to undermine your ability to do your job. This repeated intimidating and humiliating behavior threatens self-confidence, physical health, productivity, and the culture of the organization.

Very often, bullying comes from a supervisor, boss, or someone with power over the recipient. The bully assumes this person is powerless over the attacks. Bullying can be obvious or subtler, including:

- Being put down in front of others
- Sexual harassment
- Spreading rumors
- Sabotaging your work
- Taking credit for your work
- Refusing to answer your emails or calls
- Blaming you for problems
- Not acknowledging any contribution

- Harassing you with threats
- Undermining you with negative comments or sarcasm

The cost to individuals and organizations is staggering when you consider the turnover, loss of talent, and loss of momentum that occurs in organizations when bullying and disrespect become part of everyday interactions. Individuals leave jobs they once loved and experience health risks like anxiety, loss of confidence, and high blood pressure.[10]

Organizations must transform toxic behavior and manage the pain and loss experienced by their employees to stay competitive and protect their bottom line.

You cannot keep losing talented employees, fail to produce, and increase risk with more errors while still staying competitive. In a recent study by Harvard Business School, 60,000 employment records were reviewed in eleven different companies. It was discovered that terminating a toxic employee or preventing a bad hire saved twice the amount than the best worker would save.[11]

Toxic employees usually stay because the manager doesn't want to have that difficult conversation. Avoiding this problem does not make it go away; it creates bigger and more threatening challenges.

When bullying comes from your boss, it can be more challenging but not impossible to manage.

In repeated studies over decades, Ei has been the one predictor of success. This makes Ei the buffer against toxic behavior. It is through this process of strengthening Ei that good leaders become great leaders, the insurance policy against bullying behavior.

Make Ei a required competency in your department. It needs to be as important as the clinical expertise required to do the job.

Teamwork is what creates success in any organization. Today, there is greater need for cross-functional teams and interaction between departments in order to solve problems quickly.

You need a plan to deal with bullying, both as the manager and personally. Bullying continues when it is allowed to continue.

Tips to Handle a Bully

1. Do not take it personally. Bullies notoriously feel insecure, and the bullying behavior helps them make up for their shortcomings. Even though the behavior is directed at you and impacts you, it is not personal. The problem is within the bully.

   They may trigger something within you that creates your reaction. There may be jealousy or they feel inadequate around you or threatened because you are moving ahead and they are stuck. The best defense is to recognize they have the problem.

   This will strengthen you and help you detach from their biting remarks.

2. Get out of the victim mentality. Bullies choose people they believe they can intimidate. Do not play into their hand. If they play a prank or tell a joke at your expense, laugh it off. Ignore them

and walk away. Remember, you have the power to set boundaries.

3. Keep a journal and write out what has happened. In one column, be objective and write down the facts. In another column, write out how this makes you feel. In a third column, write out what this reminds you of from your past.

4. Learn to deal with stress and get help dealing with the emotional stress of being bullied.

5. Talk to your boss about what is happening. Keep to the facts rather than focusing on the emotional toll it is taking on you.

6. Call the bully out. Let them know they are bullying you and question their motives. You could say: "I know you are doing this to undermine my work. Why would you do that to someone who is not hurting you?"

THE C.A.R.E DIFFERENCE™ FOR BULLYING

Keeping in mind that the bullying behavior says more about the bully, use the four steps of C.A.R.E.:

C: Connect. Go within and recognize how this behavior affects you. Keep a journal and put the facts in one column and how it impacts you in another. Remember, the bully has the problem of insecurity, even if it is your boss. It may be triggering your own insecurity, which is causing your reaction.

A: Awareness. Tap into the triggers that are being tripped with this bullying. Does it remind you of something in your past? Do you need to deal with some emotional baggage? What steps will you take to address this need and help yourself manage these emotions?

R: Resilience. Bullying creates tension and triggers the stress reaction. Engage in strategies every day to activate your resilience. Practice mindfulness, use heart-focused breathing, and unhook from the bullies attempt to catch you off guard and bring you down.

E: Empower. What resources need to be accessed? Talk to your boss, Human Resources, or other avenues that may be in place to take the issue of bullying up the chain of command. As you engage in these steps, you will distance yourself from the victim mentality that can get triggered.

As the Manager: Suggestions to Handle Bullying:

1. Deal with it immediately. If you see it, document what you saw and address it with that individual. If you have a Performance Review process, write that person a warning. Provide your staff with the policy and the process of writing up a bullying incident.

2. As the manager, it is up to you to set the tone for your department. Describe what you do want using a positive description. Rather than state, "Bullying is unacceptable," indicate that civility, courtesy, and kindness are the expected tone for interactions. Make this part of your brand, and model this for people.

    Too often, there are sacred cows in the organization that are immune to any consequences for their bullying behavior. This undermines culture more than most leaders realize. It is like having a cold and not doing anything to support a healthy immune system and letting it progress into pneumonia, sepsis, or even death.

Deal with bullying when it happens.

3. Gossip is the precursor to bullying. The word gossip comes from "go sip," when the King told his spies to go into the pubs and listen to what people were saying about him. They would report back to the king, and the people then faced the consequences of talking about the King.

   Unless you manage gossip the same as bullying, it will erode team spirit and productivity. We have all done it and been witness to it. It only undermines someone's reputation, and by listening to it, you condone it.

   Make a commitment to end gossip.

Suggestions to End Gossip

1. Walk away if someone starts gossiping.
2. Do not repeat things you have heard.
3. Do not judge others based on what you have heard.
4. Say positive things about people. Model the behavior you want to see.

The focus of this guide is everyday Ei. Next, I want to talk about styles of communication that can undermine relationships and what results.

SARCASM (YEAH, RIGHT!)

In an online dictionary, sarcasm is defined as "the use of irony to mock or convey contempt." The origin of the word is Greek and means "to tear flesh."

Sarcasm is not the same as being ironic or witty. Witty can be a play on words ("with great power comes a great electric bill").

Irony is saying something the opposite of what you mean ("I love being home with my sick child this week") Irony *can* be sarcastic; however, sarcasm tends to be biting and intended to embarrass the other person.

Any parent of teenagers has probably been the brunt of sarcasm as teens learn to push the boundaries of their feelings in conversation. "Yeah, right," may be the standard answer. You may have attempted to motivate your teen by saying, "Can you tell me how you are able to keep this room so clean?"

Interestingly, research has shown the activity in the brain is more engaged with the use of sarcasm, as the subtlety in the message has to be interpreted first. Tone, facial expression (or lack thereof), and words are all evaluated for meaning, and it takes different parts of the brain to understand.

There are cultural differences in the understanding of sarcasm. If there are any brain injuries, the individual may not get the meaning behind the use of the sarcasm. Some research has demonstrated an increase in creativity due to the increase in use of abstract thinking when sarcasm is used.[12]

Is sarcasm good or bad? Rather than put sarcasm into these categories, think about the outcome you want in your communication. Using humor and sarcasm can be friendly and can help people get through a tough situation at work. More than likely, in this situation, irony is more in play.

Sarcasm can truly hurt individuals and has been found to be more damaging than outright criticism. Think about how your use of sarcasm is perceived:

1. Does it get you the response you want?
2. Do people walk away not knowing what to feel?
3. Does it increase or decrease the trust people have in you?

This brings us to the next style of communicating that may underlie the harshness behind sarcasm.

PASSIVE-AGGRESSIVENESS (WHATEVER!)

This describes behavior ranging from meek, mild, and passive to angry and hostile. It is a complex coping mechanism and is unfortunately prevalent in many workplaces. Most people have either been exposed to or act in a passive-aggressive way.

This is not really surprising given the bias against expressing anger and the cultural demands to smile no matter what. This is an acceptable way to communicate in some families and work cultures. However, it does tend to wreak havoc, making it difficult to get things done.

Beginning in early childhood, this learned pattern of behavior is how some people hide their anger in a distorted attempt to manage it.

What makes this behavior so difficult is that anger is not obvious. There is usually cooperation on the surface and an effort to be "nice."

Instead of verbally expressing anger or resentment, the individual may seem agreeable and then not follow through on tasks or requests.

Here are typical passive-aggressive behaviors:

1. Lack of follow-through and saying, "I forgot."
2. Blaming others for what they did.
3. "I'm not mad," or "I'm fine," then walking away, shutting down any further discussion.
4. Saying one thing and doing another. Have you had someone say, "I will do it," or, "I am coming," and then nothing happens?
5. "I was only joking," or, "Why are you getting so upset?" often comes after a sarcastic comment is not received with a smile. The individual doesn't want to own or openly acknowledge their feelings, and when they see a negative reaction in others, they can act shocked and critical of the "overreaction."
6. Backhanded compliments like, "You have done so well for your age [your size, education, you name it]," are confusing at best and usually deeply hurtful.
7. People who engage in passive aggressiveness frequently procrastinate. This can be a meth-

od to get out of doing something they don't want to do.

8. "You just want everything to be perfect." Doing the job in an inferior way and blaming others for "wanting it perfect" is another way of demonstrating this behavior.

Let's look at an example.

You decide to bring your lunch to work to eat healthy and not have to spend time in the cafeteria in long lines. Labeled and dated, you put your lunch in the refrigerator. That day, the sales representatives bring lunch in, so you do not eat your bagged lunch.

The next day, you do not bring lunch because you know you have something already at work. The previous night, one of the night staff decided to eat your lunch "because it was there" and they were hungry.

This happened even with a stated policy to not eat food that is labeled and dated. When you approach this person to talk this out, you hear, "What's the big deal? It was only a sandwich. I'll buy you lunch sometime." With a big smile and a condescending glance, they turn and walk away.

Do you run after the person shouting at them, "Keep your grimy mitts off my food!" or do you smile and say, "I am sure you were hungry, and I am glad you could enjoy my sandwich," thinking of ways to sabotage them later? Or, do you seethe with anger and then take it out on the next person who crosses your path?

This behavior is frustrating because the ambiguous communication makes it difficult to be sure what someone's motives really are. The nature of the behavior is to hide true feelings.

What can you do if you are the recipient of passive-aggressiveness?

Set boundaries.

This is another skill that is difficult for people, which may be another reason why this behavior pattern is so prevalent. Even if you are not acting passive-aggressive, if you enable this person by picking up the slack or avoiding confrontation by not saying anything, you are contributing to the problem.

Remember the section on the "Drama" conversations?

We are always one hundred percent responsible for our feelings, whether we acknowledge them or not. The risk of ignoring your feelings is that the anger the passive-aggressive person doesn't express gets acted out by the recipient of the behavior.

Boundaries are how we let other people know how we want to be treated. By not saying anything, you are giving that person permission to treat you any way they want. If you act out in anger, you risk your reputation at work and will probably end up feeling bad about yourself. And you do not change anything.

In the case of the stolen lunch, you could take the person aside the next time you see them and follow the C.A.R.E Difference™ model.

THE C.A.R.E. DIFFERENCE™ FOR PASSIVE-AGGRESSIVENESS

It could go something like this:

Connect: Start with yourself: recognize that you have a right to stand up for yourself. You should also connect with the other person, recognizing there may have been an extenuating circumstance explaining their behavior. Be open.

Awareness. Tune in to your own triggers and know when your anger switch is tripped. Identify how the situation makes you feel.

Resilience. Recognize your feelings may put you in the fight-or-flight stress mode, and engage in heart-focused breathing, relax your body, and open your perspective.

Empower. When you talk with that person, open the conversation using "I" statements: "When *I* realized my lunch was gone, *I* was stunned because *I* thought we were all working together. It was busy, and *I* was really hungry. There was little time to get anything to eat."

Demonstrate your connection with the other person by expressing empathy: "I understand you may have also been busy and did not have time to order food. I want to be able to trust that my food will be there the next day. What can you do to have a back-up plan to eat when you work nights?"

You have stated your feelings, having owned them first and then set limits based on your mutual working relationship. You have also made this person responsible for figuring out the problem rather than you coming up with a solution.

When working with a passive-aggressive person, it is important for you to have clear and consistent boundaries. This helps this person understand acceptable behavior since they lack this ability to understand how they impact others with their behavior. When you are in a culture that accepts passive-aggressiveness, boundaries may backfire because this level of direct communication will be perceived as threatening.

Here is where you have to make a decision: do you compromise your healthy communication to get along? I have seen this happen in my coaching practice where very competent professionals end up acting in passive aggressive ways themselves only to lose confidence and have their self-esteem erode.

This doesn't serve anyone. Engaging in healthy communication is a process in which you learn how to approach each other. I believe it is part of your responsibility to your career to explore other work options and keep these in your back pocket. You do not want to dismiss passive-aggressiveness as "no big deal" and then wake up one day and feel trapped by it.

Boundaries also include knowing the types of behaviors or experiences you want in your life. Are you willing and ready to work in a setting that is respectful?

Tips to Deal with Passive-Aggressiveness

1. You are not responsible for how someone treats you. This behavior says more about them. You cannot control how someone acts, and you did

not cause the reaction. Remembering this will help you avoid an overreaction.

2. Use the facts and avoid opinions. For example, your boss walked by you this morning and they were not smiling. This is a fact. An opinion or emotional reaction would be, "My boss is angry with me."

3. State your boundaries clearly and consistently in a calm and respectful way (what is acceptable and not acceptable behavior in relating to you).

4. Use the C.A.R.E. model to walk through your approach to this person. This four-step process helps you connect within, name your feelings, and then take action while empowering both you and the other person with a positive solution.

5. It is important to reflect on the times you may have been passive-aggressive yourself. Maybe someone asked you to do something, and you didn't want to do it but didn't feel like you could say no, so you delayed getting it done. Have you ever called in sick instead of facing a conflict? This is not to blame anyone—the point here is to be honest with *yourself* about your feelings.

6. Become more self-aware of triggers for anger or resentment, and deal with your anger. I have an exercise on the next page that is useful.

7. Practice mindfulness. Check out that section along with the *Attention Reboot*.

Individuals who regularly express passive-aggressive behavior do not feel it is safe, acceptable, or useful to directly express their anger and instead hold it inside. It is advisable to get coaching to help you identify and express feelings so you can enjoy healthier and more satisfying relationships.

REFLECTION

Write out your triggers.

I get angry when:

_____
_____
_____
_____
_____
_____

I choose to feel this instead:

_____
_____
_____
_____
_____
_____

**Say what you mean;
don't be mean saying it.**

HIGHLY SENSITIVE?

While highly sensitive people make up about twenty percent of the population, these *normal* traits are not well understood. The author of the book *Highly Sensitive People* shares research demonstrating that this trait is also present in other species, including cats, dogs, fruit flies, fish, and many more.[13]

Highly sensitive people:

- Notice more details and subtleties. They also can get overwhelmed more easily because of this.
- Think and feel more deeply. They reflect and make associations and by doing so, they are more apt to learn from situations by thinking about them and reviewing their experiences. Emotions have been found to contribute to learning and motivation.
- Have more active intuition
- Are bothered by loud noises and can be startled easily.
- Do not like to be disturbed when concentrating.
- Can overreact.
- Have one sense that is more acute than others.

If you have these characteristics, you need to recognize it and begin to take care of yourself in the workplace.

Often, highly sensitive people are told, "Get over it. You are too sensitive," and can end up feeling inadequate or distressed. Go back and read the section on bullying. Do not take these comments personally. Learn more about being highly sensitive and take care of yourself.

Educate others and let them know what your experience is like using "I" statements. Also, keep in mind that you will have to find ways to adapt. Your awareness of these sensitivities will help you step out of the victim mentality, even if others seem to be picking on you.

Find a trusted friend who can help you interpret behavior and do a "reality check" on how someone is responding to you. Over time, it is possible to develop thicker skin and learn to go with the flow!

ASSERTIVENESS

My graduate thesis for my master's degree studied the moderating effects of assertiveness on burnout. Using assertive communication did reduce the impact of stress. By learning this skill and becoming more assertive, you can reduce the stress you experience!

Assertiveness is misunderstood and difficult for many. In this section, we are going to explore what gets in the way of being assertive. This is often confused with getting your own way or standing up for yourself, *whether they like it or not.*

Assertive behavior is somewhere between passive and aggressive. It is your ability to stand up for yourself while also respecting other people. It doesn't always feel good to be assertive, depending on your comfort zone; however, the outcome is better. You will increase your confidence, decrease the stress you experience, and build influence among your followers and peers.

Do you consider yourself to be assertive?

Rate yourself 1–10 with 10 being consistently assertive.

1   2   3   4   5   6   7   8   9   10

At the foundation of assertiveness is your ability to value yourself and your strengths.

Tips to Develop Your Assertiveness

1. Your opinions, thoughts, and needs are *just as important* as someone else's. This doesn't mean you are more important and "deserve" to have things your way; that would be an aggressive attempt at manipulation. And you are not *less* important, which would be taking a passive way out.

   Being assertive doesn't mean you do not feel some nervousness as you speak up. It simply means you recognize that it is your responsibility to take charge and speak up for yourself—even when it makes you nervous.

   At times, you may decide, asserting yourself is not worth it and just go along to get along. If you end up feeling devalued as a result, you may want to question your passive communication style.

2. Know what you like and what you don't. Are you clear on your preferences? This keeps you from being wishy-washy, and it also helps you go after what you want.

3. Express yourself while respecting others. Recently, I attended a conference and witnessed the following: a woman seated at the end of the row was joined by two people who sat down next to her. Immediately, the woman at the end of the row said, "Your perfume is giving me a severe headache. I am nauseous. Would you sit somewhere else?"

   The couple who sat down was obviously upset when confronted like this and quickly moved to another seat in the row behind this woman. The woman on the end of the row promptly got up and left the room, only to return shortly after and reclaim her seat.

   I was shocked at this woman's abrupt and aggressive style. While in theory she was standing up for herself, she also diminished the couple (and herself) in the process. It is true that having chemical sensitivities can be difficult; however, she could have easily gotten up and changed her seat rather than embarrassing the couple. This would have created a win-win for everyone.

   Assertiveness creates win-win opportunities instead of shutting down dialogue.

4. Learn to say no. Clarity is a powerful thing! Do you know what needs your focus the most? Not having clear priorities and wanting to please people locks you into saying yes when you really should say no.

Learning to say no will give you the space and energy to say yes to what you really want to do.

When asked to do something that is not your priority or that you do not have time for, say something like, "Thank you for the offer, but I am swamped at this time."

If you want time to think about it, you can say, "Thanks for thinking of me; I need to get back to you tomorrow morning. Does this work for you?"

What keeps you from being assertive? Write it out:

_____

_____

_____

_____

Barriers to Being Assertive

Wanting to be liked (or loved) by everyone will interfere with your ability to stand up for yourself. This includes being recognized by everyone. Being kind and being assertive is not mutually exclusive. Keep in mind that people who are passive-aggressive will not like your assertiveness, and overly passive people will object when you assert yourself.

What is important is to be true to your values, needs, and desires. If not, other people's opinions will define your esteem and break down your confidence.

Perfectionism is another barrier to being assertive. How can you stand up for yourself when there is a risk of failure?

Needing to be right. In this case, you are likely to be more aggressive and insist everyone adopt your way of thinking.

Ambivalence. Are you clear on your goal? Do you know the direction you want to go? Clarity will help you be more confident and assertive.

THE C.A.R.E DIFFERENCE™ FOR ASSERTIVENESS

C: Connect within and identify your values, goals, needs, and desires. Write these out in a journal.

Decide you will also connect with the other person as opposed to avoiding them or using manipulation to get your way.

A: Awareness. Tune in to how you feel when you need to speak up for yourself. Are certain situations easier or harder?

Keep a journal and list all the times you were successful in speaking up. Also, look at the times you failed to speak up. What were your thoughts at that time?

R: Resilience. Engage in mindfulness practices every day. Use the heart-focused breathing technique, the Attention Reboot, or mindful eating to build your resilience. This will make you less susceptible to a runaway stress reaction.

E: Empower. Use all resources available to increase your confidence and identify your strengths. Engage the other person in problem solving and create a win-win opportunity if possible. If you decide you have to agree to disagree, respect the relationship.

This approach is also a reminder to take care of yourself. People pleasing, rescuing, and being a victim is exhausting and steals your professional collateral.

Practice assertiveness with a trusted friend, in front of the mirror, and in small ways at work to continue to build this skill. The risk is much bigger if you continue to play small and not speak up.

10. CLICHÉS AND IDIOMS

Cliché is a French word that comes out of the printing industry; it is the sound made when a printing plate moved. That plate was called a "stereotype" plate. Today, the word cliché describes a phrase that denotes a common thought.

These phrases can be overused, such as *back in the day.* This could mean, "I am so experienced, I remember when the wheel was invented. So, you cannot tell me anything I do not know." Or, it could mean that you long for the "good old days" and would rather keep things the same.

The point of thinking about what and how you say something is to reflect on the objective of your communication. What is the outcome you want from the conversation or interaction?

Common Clichés

Time will tell—can be perceived as evasive or unclear.

As old as the hills—can send a message that you are sensitive about your age.

Waking up on the wrong side of the bed—interestingly enough, this sends the message that you do not have control over your emotions or that you do not care how you impact others.

There is no "I" in "team"—may be intended to motivate people to work together because "**teamwork makes the dream work.**" It can also mean that stepping outside of the box and ahead of the team is not appreciated. This only dulls the stars in the group.

If you want the team to work better together, then say that. "When the team works together, we get further ahead faster." Ideally, use measurable terms, so everyone knows what "further" and "faster" means.

Work smarter, not harder—I have a program called Work S.M.A.R.T. and I like this phrase. I also understand that when people hear this, they may be bracing themselves for having to do even more than they do now in less time.

People usually use clichés when there is little time to explain what you really mean. However, it is best to say exactly what you mean. "Work smarter" becomes, "When you avoid things that drain energy like worry, you can get more done."

Perception is reality—This might work for an abstract thinker, but what about the person who is more concrete? It is true that we all have filters through which we perceive the actual events of the day. These filters can distort the way one experiences what is happening.

Instead of this confusing phrase, try this: "We all see the world through our own lens." Ask more questions before jumping to conclusions to better understand the lens through which someone sees their world.

It is what it is—Hmm? Is this passive-aggressive? Is it an excuse to not try harder? Or, is it simply acknowledging that things are the way they are?

In the words of Sigmund Freud, "Sometimes a cigar is just a cigar." What this means is that these phrases are not always bad, but it is the emotional undertone and or the hidden meaning that is slipped in when trying to be cute that distorts the message.

The point is to be more aware of what you feel and then be deliberate with what you want to say. Finally, look for the evidence that your message has had the impact you intended.

Idioms are just like clichés: people misinterpret the phrase because of the emotional undertone and the delivery of it.

An idiom is a collection of words that has a different meaning than the words themselves. For example, "it's raining cats and dogs" is not to be taken literally.

Both clichés and idioms are interpreted differently by people, and it is difficult to know just how someone may perceive what you are saying. Your body language, tone of voice, facial expression, and the receiver's history with this phrase become part of the message. It is easy to send a mixed signal when you rely on clichés and idioms to communicate. Unless you know the individual and have established a history, using these phrases is risky in everyday communication.

It is easy to hide behind a phrase with a hint of sarcasm or hidden anger. Check out this reflection exercise and do a self-check.

REFLECTION

Think about how you use these common phrases.

Are you sarcastic when you use them?

_____

_____

_____

Are you being passive-aggressive? Are you jabbing someone without actually saying it?

_____

_____

_____

What is your intention as you use the phrase?

_____

_____

The more aware you become of your own triggers and when you feel angry, the better you'll be at keeping your message clear of any hidden emotions.

11. BODY LANGUAGE

We all have been frustrated, bored, or upset at meetings or during conversations at work. Do you know how it impacts your body language and your communication?

Ei is increasing your awareness of what you are feeling and how these emotions may play out in what and how you communicate. Knowing how you impact others is also a component of Ei.

In this section, tune in to your body language and how this may (or may not) be advancing your message of confidence. There are great books[14] that go into detail about what all these gestures mean and how you can use them to increase rapport and engagement. For the scope of this book, I want you to notice how your feelings may be impacting your body language. Think in terms of when you are relaxed or not. What happens in your body?

We can probably all agree that the stress reaction creates tension. When this instinct is triggered, your body chooses to fight, freeze, or flee unless you have learned to activate resilience and interrupt the reaction.

Look at this chart and make a note of how your body responds.

Gesture	What Are You Feeling?	Match Feeling with Gesture
Slouching; shoulders hunched		Confident
Hands wringing; fidgety		Self-doubt
Yawning		Angry
Crossing arms		Scared
Eye roll		Confused
Turning one's back		Focused
Straight posture		Intimidated
Leaning in; eye contact		Ready
Clenched fist		Prepared
Smiling, joking		Tired
Facing the individual		Bored
		Cynical

SAY THIS... NOT THAT.

REFLECTION

Think about your body language. Do you:

- ❏ Slump
- ❏ Slouch
- ❏ Make eye contact
- ❏ Turn your back
- ❏ Yawn
- ❏ Check your phone
- ❏ Check your watch
- ❏ Frown excessively
- ❏ Roll your eyes
- ❏ Other: _____

Remember that while you may not have any negative intention behind these behaviors, they are communicating something.

Is it the message you want people to get about you?

_____
_____
_____

12. TRY SAYING THIS INSTEAD

The following are commonly used phrases. While they may not hijack your message when used occasionally, become aware of how often you use them, the emotion underneath, and if they are actually conveying the message you intend.

"This is probably not what you want to hear."

If your first thought is this, then you have to revise your message. If you want to put people on the defensive and set up barriers to understanding, say this. If not say this instead:

1. State the facts.
2. Do not delay in getting the message out. This avoids surprise, which no one likes.
3. Justify what you are saying. Make the case.
4. Find the silver lining.
5. Empathize. Acknowledge that this is tough for people and you understand.

"I guess it just wasn't meant to be."

This depends on how you say it and in what context. If someone is upset about a missed opportunity, this can be perceived as insensitive, even if you did not mean it to come off this way.

How do you know what is meant to be? Is there sarcasm in this message? Double check what is going on inside of you.

Instead, consider saying this:

1. "I can see you are upset. I am sorry this happened."
2. Acknowledge the person's experience. Make eye contact; this lets them know you care.

"We're experiencing a paradigm shift."

Huh? Use clear language to say what you mean.

Try this instead:

"We need a new model for this." Then, spell it out clearly.

"It's not fair."

After kindergarden, this is no longer appropriate. It makes you look powerless and blames the other person. Get beyond the feeling and think about what you really want to say, sticking to facts.

Try this instead: "Five other people were chosen to work nights, and they were all the new hires. I am the only one with seniority. Can you help me understand this decision?"

You are stating numbers, facts, and specifics and sincerely want to better understand what you heard instead of placing blame.

Review the section on optimism. This phrase is a pessimist's point of veiw.

"I have no idea what is going on."

Really? Even if you meant this in a funny way, everyone may laugh, but they *will* see you in a different light afterwards.

Instead, consider this:

"Wow, would you look at that."

This will give you time to formulate a solid response.

"I don't know."

Consider saying this instead:

1. "I do not have that info and will get it."
2. "I know someone who does know this; let's contact them now."
3. "Let's brainstorm."

"We don't have sufficient boots on the ground."

Unless you are in the military, military metaphors are going to be misunderstood and not well received.

"Let's just get it done and apologize later."

I understand this may be said to motivate a quick response to a challenge, but the underlying message is that it is okay to cut corners. This is the equivalent to saying one thing and doing another; it will undermine trust in your leadership and productivity in the long run.

Try saying this instead:

1. "We need to get this done now, and it requires approval. I will put in an emergency call."

2. "How can we do this and stay within the required limits?"

"Failure is not an option."

This can be motivating to a degree, but it can also shut down any type of dialogue about how to achieve your goal. It can also send the message that it is okay to do "whatever it takes."

"Let's not try to reinvent the wheel."

The status quo is okay, then?

"I don't care."

Is that correct? Try this: say nothing. You are just revealing your loss of patience and a passive-aggressive attitude.

"You're wrong."

This is like a red flag to a bull. Try this instead:

"There are many ways to do this. Tell me more." Seek to understand the reason behind that person's method.

"You can't do it."

Discouraging and blunt. Withhold judgement; it only creates resentment. Show curiosity and interest. Ask questions and encourage this person to demonstrate their thought process. Let them come to the conclusion that another way may be better.

"As I said before . . ."

No one wants this reminder. It comes off as smug, arrogant, and a put down. Simply repeat your instructions or comments.

"Good luck!"

Remember the section on sarcasm and passive-aggressive behavior? Try this instead: "I know you have this!"

"I'll try."

Actually, there are only two choices—"I will" or "I won't." Be decisive and make a commitment. Try this instead: "I look forward to the challenge."

"This might sound stupid, but. . ."

Playing small and undermining yourself is not the way to stand out. Recognizing you don't know something is a demonstration of strength. Try this instead: note that you feel vulnerable and this makes you insecure. Breathe deeply and release that insecure feeling, then ask your question.

"You look good for your age."

This is a backhanded compliment or a sign that you are socially impaired. Either way, it is like a lead balloon and will dampen any mood. Try this: "You look great!"

"I could never wear that."

Passive-aggressive. What are you really saying and what is your feeling underneath it? Jealousy, envy, disgust—what? How does this advance your relationship?

"Could be worse!"

This is a closet pessimist's favorite saying. "Not bad" is right up there with it. Be positive. You may even notice that you feel better when your response is, "I am great."

"I need you to focus."

Indeed. And the more distracted one gets, the more specific instruction is required. This can carry an edge of sarcasm and smugness to it. It can be code for, "What's the matter with you?"

Try this: use your hand gestures to demonstrate where you want the focus, or if you want their attention, say, "I need you to listen in as there are a lot of details to cover."

"You look angry."

You are not a bullfighter, so do not wave that red cape. It may be best to say nothing. If they are angry, the timing is not good for a conversation.

"You look upset. What did I do?"

Similar to the phrase above, this can be provocative. When you state this in a different way, you are coming from your own point of view, taking the pressure off the other person to defend themselves.

Try this instead: "I am concerned I may have said something to upset you."

"As long as it takes."

I doubt very sincerely that you mean that. Is it really okay for your new manager to take "all the time in the world" to learn how to do this new thing? While this may be meant to be encouraging, it is weak and does not provide any parameters or set expectations. Be specific and give measurable limits.

Try this instead: "I support you as you learn this new role. I want that report by Friday next week, June 6. Does this work for you?"

"You look tired."

Hmm . . . this is likely to raise some defensiveness. Try this instead: "Everything okay?"

"You have lost so much weight."

Weight is like politics and religion: it is not a subject one brings up unless invited to do so. And I still would not discuss it. Try this instead: "You look great," or, "You look refreshed."

"It is up to you, whatever you want."

This is passive and can make you look like you do not care or you are not interested in the activity or individual.

Try this instead: "I am looking forward to spending time with you and insist you pick the restaurant." Or, give your preferences: "I like Greek and Italian."

"I told you so."

Resist this. It never turns out well.

"It is not in my job description."

What are you really saying? And what are you feeling? Angry? If your boss asks you to do something, it would be in your best interest to find a way to accommodate them if you want to advance your career and build up favor.

Try this instead: if time is an issue, say, "I would love to help you out except I have two post-ops coming in and I am supposed to be there for them."

This gives the boss a chance to negotiate or arrange for alternatives. If it is something you do not have the skills to do, try, "I do not have the skills to do this."

Keep the conversation open rather than shutting it down with this statement. If this is chronic, then look for another job. Think about the impact on you and your future when you respond.

Responding out of anger always requires damage control to your reputation. Is it worth it?

"I hate this job."

Then look for another one and do not say a word. Find ways to release your anger, disappointment, or other emotions in a place that is safe and will not have negative consequences for you. Take care of yourself.

This is like a toxic gas that affects your coworkers and destroys morale, and it will back fire on you, possibly alienating your coworkers and destroying any chance for future promotions.

"He's stupid/lazy/incompetent."

Name calling is never going to advance your cause in a positive way. Once you hear this going on in your head, it is time to do a self-check. Chances are you are stressed out and in the fight-or-flight reaction. Perspective is shortsighted and reactive.

Use the *Count of Four* breathing, generate feelings of gratitude, and shift from a survival mode to be able to see possibilities.

When at work, it is more productive to see challenges using a systemic point of view versus blaming people for the outcomes. Step back and evaluate what the processes are that need changing.

If a person has behavior that is destroying morale or productivity, then use the system that is in place to move them out of your department or organization.

Name calling sets up a toxic environment and destroys trust, morale, and productivity. Set a standard for civility and respect and hold people accountable.

13. EVERYDAY MINDFULNESS

I first wrote this in *Resilience: Your Super Power*.[15]

We live in the Age of Distraction. Bringing mindfulness into your day will help you enjoy greater satisfaction in your work and improve your ability to communicate in a healthy, positive way.

Research into the power of the brain now demonstrates that the brain can change in response to what we think, feel, and do. The brain function and structure can change with a regular practice of mindfulness. Research has shown changes in concentration, overall wellbeing, memory, anxiety, sleep, and self-esteem, to name a few of the many benefits of a mindfulness practice.

This neuroplasticity is good and bad. If you keep reacting and doing what you have always done, it is easier to keep doing this. This is how habits are quickly formed: when you are distracted and continue to operate based on a knee-jerk decision. Mindfulness increases your awareness and will slow down your reactive decisions.

As you go through your busy day wrapped up in thoughts and feelings without a break, you may find it useful to check in. Stop and ask yourself, "What is happening right now, in this moment?"

Mindfulness Is a Form of Meditation

Mindfulness means directing your attention to what is happening in the moment without any type of judgement. This takes practice because the mind has a steady stream of thoughts, feelings, and questions and quickly goes off track. Mindfulness is the practice of bringing your focus into the moment while tuning out the competing thoughts and feelings.

This practice increases your ability to focus and decreases your reactivity to stress. As you tune in, you are observing your experience rather than reacting to it. This means you simply notice what you are experiencing without trying to change what you are experiencing.

Start By Setting Your Intention

Intention is where you direct your attention. This is the first step in a mindfulness practice. You have to first set a goal that you will be present. Your intention references where you will be directing your attention.

When you are mindful, you are bringing your attention back to your goal, over and over.

1. Set your intention.
2. Stay aware of this intention.
3. As you notice thoughts, feelings, and other distractions, remind yourself of your intention and redirect your attention.

These three steps are the foundation of your mindfulness practice. Use these to increase your ability to be present and focused during everyday activities.

SAY THIS... NOT THAT.

Mindful Eating

Let's say it is your intention (goal) to be present while you eat. With lives on the go, fast food has become the norm. Over seventy-five percent of food that is eaten is processed and already prepared. This is only part of the problem; this food is eaten in a car, in front of the TV or computer, or while reading. You can double your caloric intake when you eat this way, as your body does not feel full in time to register what you have eaten.

Next time you eat (and it doesn't matter what you eat), start by taking a few deep breaths: in on a count of four, hold on a count of four, and then out on a count of four. Then, continue to breathe for about ten seconds. This should quiet your mind and help you focus on your food.

As you eat, notice the weight of the food on the fork, or the color, aroma, and textures of the food as you look at it on your plate. Chew each bite and notice what is happening in your mouth as you chew. Just focus on your experience as you eat. It is normal for your mind to wander as you start this practice; simply notice and remind yourself of your intention to be present while you eat, then bring your attention back to your food.

By eating slower and tuned in to yourself, you will recognize more quickly when you feel satisfied. Stop eating before you feel full. Your stomach digests best when it is two-thirds full. Wrap up the rest of your food and push away from the table. Take a few sips of water to refresh your palette, and breathe deeply for ten seconds.

Mindfulness is an exercise you can practice at any time. Use your breath to bring you back to a quiet place so you can keep your attention on what is going on in the moment. Keep your journal handy, as you may find yourself gaining insights into your choices and behavior.

Suggestions to Apply Mindfulness in Your Day

The following are ways you can incorporate mindfulness into your day. Choose one to use for a few days, and then add in others as this practice becomes easier. Consistency with this practice will yield tremendous benefit (versus longer periods of practice done infrequently).

1. Before you get out of bed, take a deep breath. Breathe in gratitude and out frustration for ten seconds.
2. Drink six ounces of water. Notice how you feel after drinking the water. Refreshed?
3. When brushing your teeth, notice the weight of the toothpaste. Any color or smell? What is the temperature of the paste as your brush your teeth? Keep your thoughts on the activity of brushing your teeth. Notice the temperature of the water. How does your mouth feel after brushing? When finished, look at yourself in the mirror and smile!
4. While driving to work, start with noticing the car. What color is it? Is it dirty or clean? Do you open with it a key fob? What does that sound like? Do you press it once or twice? As you slide into the seat, what does the texture feel like?

When you start the engine, how does it sound? Running smoothly? Any chugging sounds? As you drive to work, keep your thoughts on the driving experience. Notice the cars as they come up on you. Use your mirrors and be fully present to driving. As your mind wanders onto thoughts about what you have to do at work, bring your attention back to driving. Use the word *driving* to keep your attention on this experience.

When you pull into work and park, before you turn off the engine, notice how you feel. Take a deep breath. Are you more relaxed?

5. Before you go into a meeting, set an intention to be fully present. As you walk down the hall to the meeting, what do you notice? How are you feeling? Who do you see? What is on the walls? On the floor? What noises or smells are there?

    When you get into the meeting, keep your mind on what is happening in the meeting. When your mind wanders to lunch or your vacation or any other subject, bring yourself back to the meeting.

    How do you feel when the meeting ends and what did you notice that is new?

6. Eating. Use the mindfulness exercise on eating and make this a "rule" for one meal a day. Be fully present when you eat.

ATTENTION REBOOT

This is a great exercise. You can use this when you feel stuck or when you notice your mood is sinking. Practice this regularly and you will develop the ability to reboot your attention quickly. It is a mindfulness practice.

1. Start with a few deep breaths and shift your mind to the present.
2. If you are in a meeting, imagine you are there for the very first time. Step back from your assumptions and just observe. Let any judgements drift out of your mind.
3. You can use this as you walk around your department or organization. Go outside your department and simply observe, being completely present to the sounds, colors, interactions. Resist making any judgements. Simply observe.
4. What did you notice that you missed in the past? Journal your observations.

Emotions are contagious. Go viral with a positive and inspiring message.

14. TRANSFORMING CONFLICT

Work would be so much easier if everyone just got along! But we all know this is not what usually happens. Tension can be high with demands and time constraints; tempers flare with the impulse to let someone have it.

Add to this tension the lack of awareness of what you are feeling and the lack of skills to have those difficult conversations. As a result, many people are not aware they are upset until they are already in a conflict with someone.

These two dimensions of Ei (emotional awareness and emotional expression) are the ones that present the biggest challenge for most people. Often during a difficult interaction, people react to what is happening, only to provoke someone's hot button, leaving both people upset.

> **Keep in mind, you are completely responsible for your feelings, even when someone else triggers them.**

Have you ever felt like this?

Kelly is late again with the report she promised last week. Brad consistently has to ask her for the information he needs to finish his work. Brad is frustrated and did not appreciate having to make an excuse to his boss because he was late with his report.

Brad is fuming about this, and when he sees Kelly in the hall, he unloads on her, "Kelly, you are always late with information. You did it again, and now I look like I can't get my work done."

Kelly reacts to Brad's anger. "I am not always late. If you would ask me on time, maybe I could get it to you." And she stomps off.

Brad yells after her, "You never take responsibility for anything!"

Their coworkers witness this exchange, leaving everyone with uncomfortable feelings and the wrong impression about Brad and Kelly.

Even though you may be upset and may even be "right," yelling at someone will not advance the conversation nor support your brand. And holding in your anger is not any better. Even if you do not yell at them, until you resolve this conflict, you will have underlying resentment, making every interaction more difficult than it needs to be.

Brad wanted Kelly to know how he felt, but with this approach, the conversation was doomed from the start. What went wrong?

Tips to Transform Conflict into Opportunity

1. Avoid using words like "always" or "never." They can provoke the other person and come off as blaming.

2. Avoid having a conversation when you are angry or seething. Own your feelings and deal with them instead of blaming the other person for them.

3. Think the best about the person with whom you want to resolve the conflict, rather than believing they are out to get you.
4. Handling conflict well will help you advance in your career.
5. Use "I" phrases and seek understanding versus spreading blame and shame.
6. If you need to develop your assertiveness, practice these suggestions in front of a mirror first or with a trusted friend.
7. Have the conversation before it loses relevance. If you wait to talk about the issue until long after it's happened, the other person may end up feeling hijacked, even if you say all the right things.
8. Avoid profanity. It is an excuse to convey emotions without substance. When you rely on the emotional tone that underlies profanity, you block your ability to identify your emotions. This inhibits a clear and effective message. It keeps you from being in control of what and how you are communicating.

Many people avoid having difficult conversations and lose the opportunity to build trust and deepen understanding. Make a commitment to develop this skill of having difficult conversations; your future success depends on it.

"You made me feel . . ."

If you start an interaction with this phrase, it can be a hot button for the person to whom you are talking and can shut down the conversation. While your feelings may seem like they are triggered by someone's action, your feelings are *your* responsibility. It is powerful (and important) for you to realize this.

Use this formula to express your feelings:

When _____ **happened (or you said** _____**), I felt** _____.

This approach will engage the other person rather than putting them off with, "You made me feel . . ." because they interpret this as you blaming them. Now you have the chance to actually dialogue and understand each other. This also requires you to name your feelings, accept your feelings as your responsibility, and then take charge of them. This is empowering!

You can approach the other person like this:

"There is something that has been bothering me, and I would like to talk with you about it."

Then use the "I" phrases and the above formula.

- I was hurt when . . .
- I was caught off guard . . .
- I was confused and . . .
- I felt betrayed when you said . . .
- I was shocked by your comment . . .
- When you did *xyz*, my brain heard you say . . .

THE C.A.R.E. DIFFERENCE™ WITH CONFLICT

C: Connect

Question for you: What am I feeling?

First, Brad connects with his feelings and acknowledges his anger. He also has a goal to connect with Kelly as opposed to blaming her.

A: Awareness

Question for you: How will I handle my feelings?

Aware of his anger, Brad makes the decision to do something about it.

He is also aware that Kelly may have something going on that is keeping her from getting the reports to him on time.

R: Resilience

Question for you: What perspective will create understanding?

Brad needs to engage his resilience instead of reacting out of the primitive survival reaction of the stress response.

The Heart-Focused Breathing technique discussed in the section on Engaging Your Body's Intelligence works well to increase your resilience and can be used in the moment to unhook from that fight-or-flight reaction.

E: Empowered

Question for you: How can I resolve this?

In this step, Brad wants to understand Kelly's side of the issue and agree on an acceptable solution. He wants understanding to build trust and strengthen their relationship, and he wants to find a resolution of the conflict so it doesn't keep happening.

Before Brad approaches Kelly, he makes sure the conversation will be private:

"Kelly, there is something that has been bothering me, and I would like to talk to you about it."

"Sure, Brad, what's up?"

"I have been reprimanded by my boss for being late with my reports. I cannot get my work done until I have the information from you."

Kelly may say, "I'm sorry, Brad, I didn't know you were waiting for me." Or, she may have an edge to her voice and respond with, "It's not my problem your boss jumped on you."

Brad responds with, "I know you're not doing this on purpose. I also know you have a lot going on. I was wondering when might be an acceptable timeline to get me this information."

In this exchange, he demonstrates empathy and is also holding her accountable.

Kelly relaxes some, knowing Brad understands. She responds, "Yes, I have to collate all the data for the month and prepare the report for the Governance Committee, and it is due the same day you want your information. I would be better off if I could get you your information a week later."

Brad wants to be clear about his need for Kelly to follow through and adds, "That will be fine, Kelly. If you find yourself in a bind again, we need a back-up plan."

This lets Kelly know that she is accountable, and as the conversation moves forward, they both have the opportunity to troubleshoot the demand and find a better solution.

Use bridge statements throughout your conversation to demonstrate empathy and close the gap from conflict to understanding.

Phrases that Bridge the Gap

I know you did not do this on purpose.

I understand (you didn't mean it to sound angry, you didn't mean to be hurtful, etc.) . . .

I understand how you see it now.

I am certain (you did not want to make me late on my work) . . .

I can see now (that you are swamped and could not get to my request) . . .

Let's work on a solution together.

Can we talk this through to understand each other (or the situation)?

Let's lay out the facts and see where we are.

Let's find common ground.

I am sorry. (*Apologies open up communication. It is not an admission you were wrong.*)

Are you happy with the compromise?

Is there something else we need to discuss?

I am happy we could resolve this (and come to an understanding).

I value our relationship.

I look forward to a solution.

It is a good idea to restate the solution so everyone can agree.

ACTIVE LISTENING

We spend the majority of our day communicating in some form. Half that time is spent listening. Unfortunately, most people do not listen well. While we talk at about 150 words per minute, our brain can take in 450 words per minute. That may explain why people jump in before someone is really finished with their response.

"I know what you are going to say." How do you feel when someone interrupts you and says this?

_____
_____
_____
_____
_____

Just because the brain can take in more than twice the words than we can speak, that doesn't mean the message can be understood in half the time. Active listening means you are engaged in the act of listening and nothing else.

Active listening includes listening to the words and observing gestures, tone, and emotional nuances while seeking understanding. Judgement is withheld and any confusion is clarified with additional questions.

Active listening is powerful; yet, it rarely happens. Check out this chart for examples of what active listening looks like.

Letting the person know you are interested	Nodding "I see what you mean." "Yes."
Encouraging the person to say more so you can better understand	"Tell me more about..." "What makes you say that?"
To clarify what was said, giving the person the chance to hear back what they said	"Okay, the problem *as you see it* is..."
To acknowledge the emotional tone of what they said	"You feel strongly that..."
To summarize specific points of agreement and disagreement	"We agree on the following..." "We need to talk more about..." (disagreements)

Listen more.

Talk less.

Observe.

15. EMPATHY

The understanding of empathy has evolved since the word's inception. Psychologist Edward B. Titchener introduced the word in 1909 to translate a German word, *Einfühlung,* meaning "feeling into." This word was used to describe the reaction to works of art and nature. Romantic thinkers at that time used the word as a way to compensate for the intellectual dissection of the elements of nature. Since then, *empathy* has gone through an evolution as researchers and social psychologists have sought to better understand its meaning.

For a time, empathy was considered the same as sympathy or pity—feeling sorry for another. Today, that is not the case, with *empathy* and *sympathy* having different meanings. Why is this important?

With the overload of information and the lack of differentiation between emotions, it is easy to get drained by the emotional experience of another. There is a tendency to "overcare" and develop burnout or compassion fatigue, a very close cousin to burnout.

While there is no one academic definition of empathy, there are many definitions floating around. I want to talk about empathy in the context of work and how to deliberately build on empathy behaviors that will enhance understanding and collaboration between people, especially when under stressful conditions.

Sympathy is defined as the perception and recognition of distress in another with a desire to fix it. The person helping is seen as stronger and more powerful while the one being helped is seen as vulnerable. You can see how this might lead to burnout if you are overwhelmed with individuals who are vulnerable and your identity is that of the powerful person.

A broad definition of empathy is the ability to react to what someone is experiencing without losing oneself in the process. Empathy is a skill that can be learned and requires these companion skills: the ability to . . .

- identify or name emotions
- have emotional accuracy
- have emotional perspective (put yourself in their shoes)
- regulate your emotions
- care about others
- engage with other people

With so many people distracted and more irritable as a result of the culture of interruption, empathy can counter the sarcasm, negativity, and bullying that has become a regular part of the workplace. When leaders demonstrate empathy, the organization gains a flexible and adaptive culture, allowing employees to experience a deeper sense of meaning in their work.

People work better together when they can relate to one another. The ability to use empathy, when needed, is a strong indicator of emotional intelligence and makes you much better at influencing outcomes.

Demonstrate Empathy

While empathy has many dimensions, the critical first step is acknowledging the other person and their feelings. This is how one *demonstrates* empathy. Taking a moment to stop, look someone in the eye, and observe what they are experiencing is lost in the almost chronic feeling of urgency most experience in the workday.

While this type of acknowledgement is powerful, it is not something you need to do in most conversations.

When Do You Want to Use Empathy?

Here are two key times when you want to acknowledge someone and demonstrate empathy:

1. the other person is experiencing emotion or speaking from the heart
2. the subject they are speaking on is important to them

Can you see how being able to use this skill can make a difference in your relationships at work?

Think about all the times you've spent your energy rehashing conversations due to misunderstanding or skewed emotions. Now you have a skill to take charge of your interactions at work. Adding empathetic acknowledgement and active listening to your communication skillset will increase trust among your peers and increase your satisfaction at work as well as in your personal relationships.

Another reason to distinguish sympathy from empathy is to protect your energy from the drain of overcaring. One of the reasons people shut down at work is to avoid overcaring because they don't know the difference between sympathy and empathy.

As you develop your own self-awareness, it contributes to your ability to relate authentically to others. The first step to demonstrating empathy is to acknowledge that person, their feelings, and what they are saying. Listening is one of those skills that most people do poorly.

Did you know most people forget half of what they hear? There is a tendency to be thinking of what you want to say rather than listening to understand.

What empathy looks like:

1. Makes eye contact
2. Does not interrupt
3. Does not try to fix the problem
4. Does not criticize
5. Nods head and indicates they understand what you are saying
6. May ask questions to better understand how the person is feeling

The chart below highlights the benefits of engaging empathy, when needed.

Everyone wins. Big benefits all around.

Person Talking	Person Acknowledging
1. Sense of appreciation and value	1. Stronger connection with talker
2. Increased insight	2. Feels good to give
3. Feels less alone	3. Avoids conflict
4. Experiences relief from difficult feelings (this may be the only "fix" that is necessary)	4. Expands experience by recognizing differences in another
5. Increased trust	

16. LET'S CONTINUE THIS CONVERSATION

What did you get from this book? Insights? Jot two things down that stand out to you:

1. _____
   _____

2. _____
   _____

Reflection is how you will improve your ability to communicate more effectively and move your conversations from telling to transformative.

Why Is This Important?

As human beings, we are motivated by emotion. Managing people has to evolve from telling people what to do to engaging them in the process. To do this, it is necessary to find out what drives behavior and inspires your team.

Emotions convey information, and this information serves as a guide to take the action that will advance your goals. The way the nervous system is hardwired, we could not make decisions if we did not have the emotional centers intact. Emotions are instinctive and right next to the primitive centers in the brain that trigger fight, flight, or freeze reactions.

This book has provided a guide to move you through emotional reactions to meaningful connection. The C.A.R.E. Difference™ is a model to help you do this.

The C.A.R.E. model helps you become self-aware; as you identify which emotion is coming up, you are guided to take some action and avoid being hijacked by an undercover emotional response. We have all had it happen—without even knowing why, you find yourself screaming or yelling in reaction to someone. There is usually embarrassment or some guilt after and maybe withdrawal, further compromising the relationship.

This book is not a script for what to say; rather, it is a tool to build the skills you need for more meaningful conversations.

Self-awareness is the Foundation of Ei

Unfortunately, people are usually forced to wake up through an external event. Getting through that experience reveals who we really are. I remember early in my career when I was laid off from a job I loved. This is what led me to launch my first consultant business.

After a year consulting—on my own, not used to the uncertainty of the revenue stream—I decided to look for a job. I was hired into a position for which I felt my education and experience was well suited. I was excited about this new position with an outpatient health center. We were launching a new community-based program. I knew what needed to happen, since I had launched my own business and learned a lot in that experience.

My manager not only did not have experience with launching new programs, but she was also new to the area. I was excited to share what I knew with her, but I soon learned that you do not lead with the solution. This personal anecdote is a good example of what can happen when you put results before relationships.

Focused only on results, I ignored the opportunity to develop a deeper relationship with my boss. She presented her vision, and knowing it was not going to turn out the way she wanted, I immediately stepped in and said, "It would work better if this happened first." My intention was to have a successful outcome and not to undermine her authority. She did not see it that way.

I was promptly fired. Had I taken the time to learn more about myself and my triggers as well as how I came across to other people, I would have known to approach the discussion from a different angle.

What I also learned about myself is that I am very creative and a problem-solver, and I work best with someone who is able to handle out-of-the-box thinking and a direct style of communicating. Had I known this, I probably would not have taken this position, recognizing the mismatch in communication and leadership style.

Being authentic doesn't mean I can ignore how my direct style may impact someone who may be the opposite of that. Fortunately, Ei improves with age! Hopefully, you will learn from your mistakes!

Training in Ei can shorten the learning curve and lessen the casualties along the way.

Ei is different from your personality. It is a set of skills that you interpret *through* your personality. The way I express assertiveness is different from how you might. To be authentic, you have to get to know yourself.

Did you know the origin of the word *authentic* is *authority*? It wasn't until the 18th century that authentic was used to mean *genuine*. You have to become the authority on yourself. Self-awareness is your ticket to getting there.

Emotions are designed to *flow* freely, and it is normal to experience the full range of emotions in the course of a day. *Flow* is the important word here; getting stuck in emotions is what happens without awareness.

Without awareness, people use bravado, a mask to hide fears and insecurities, in order to get things done. This comes at the expense of having conversations that are open and honest, risking the ability to solve big problems because everyone is afraid to speak up.

Keep in mind. you are one hundred percent responsible for understanding your emotional self and taking action to get better at expressing your emotions. Work can provide a platform to develop certain skills; however, it is up to you to make this a goal and engage the resources you need to get there (like coaching).

Imagine the engagement a workplace could have if the team were passionate about the results. This is not *just* the job of the leader, to inspire and motivate. The more you understand what motivates you, the better you are able to motivate others.

SAY THIS... NOT THAT.

Be the Change That Is Needed

Make Ei a competency for you and your team. Insist that this is part of the expectation of working in your department; people skills and healthy interactions matter as much as clinical proficiency.

GRATEFUL

DEVELOP YOUR TEAM'S COMMUNICATION SKILLS

This book is the start of a conversation around more effective communication. You can build conflict competence with your team with our program:

Transform Conflict into Opportunity

This competency-based program uses assessment, training, and coaching to build the skills needed to improve communication and confidence around conflict. Based on the C.A.R.E Method™, the four-step model for communication, your team will learn what their conflict styles are and how to broaden their approach to move through conflict to effective communication.

This can be purchased to be used by a facilitator at your organization:

www.eileadership.org/store

Or, it can be customized for an on-site program.

Let's schedule a conversation!

LET'S KEEP IN TOUCH!

Sign up for our newsletter. It offers tips and strategies to build a strong team and strengthen your leadership.

Work. Lead. Differently.
www.eileadership.org

888-71-FOCUS

drh@eileadership.org

Social Sites

LinkedIn: drcynthiahoward

Twitter: drcynthiahoward

Facebook: eileader

Mail

Ei Leadership

7322 Manatee Ave W. Ste 289

Bradenton, FL 34209

ENDNOTES

[1] Fernald, A., Marchman, V., Weisleder, A. "SES Differences in Language Processing Skill and Vocabulary Are Evident at Eighteen Months," *Developmental Science* 16, no. 2 (2013): 234–48.

[2] Uhls, Y., Michikyan, M., Morris, J., et al., "Five Days at Outdoor Education Camp Without Screens Improves Preteen Skills with Nonverbal Emotional Cues," *Computers in Human Behavior*. 39 (2014): 387–92.

[3] Dadds MR1, Allen JL, Oliver BR, Faulkner N, Legge K, Moul C, Woolgar M, Scott S. "Love, eye contact and the developmental origins of empathy v. psychopathy." *Br J Psychiatry*. 2012 Mar;200(3):191–6.

[4] Tamir, D., Mitchell, J. "Disclosing information about the self is intrinsically rewarding." *PNAS* vol. 109 no. 21, May 22, 2012.

[5] Bradberry, T., Greaves, J (2009) *Emotional Intelligence 2.0*. Talentsmart: San Diego.

[6] Karpman MD, Stephen (1968). "Fairy tales and script drama analysis." *Transactional Analysis Bulletin*. 26 (7): 39–43.

[7] Howard, C. (2016) *Resilience: Your Super Power, A Practical Guide for High Performance Leadership*. Vibrant Radiant Health.

[8] HeartMath is a registered trademark of the Institute of HeartMath.

[9] Ruiz, Miguel. *The Four Agreements: A Toltec Wisdom Book*. San Rafael: Amber-Allen Pub., 1997.

[10] Gary Namie, PhD, Research Director. 2014 WBI U.S. Workplace Bullying Survey. February 2014

[11] Houseman, M., Minor, D. (2015) *Toxic Workers*. Working Paper. Harvard Business School.

[12] Huang, L.; Gino, F.; Galinsky, A.D. (2015). "The Highest Form of Intelligence: Sarcasm Increases Creativity Through Abstract Thinking for Both Expressers and Recipients." *Organizational Behavior and Human Decision Processes*.

[13] Aron, E. (2013) *The Highly Sensitive Person: How To Thrive When The World Overwhelms You*. Citadel.

[14] Navarro, J., Sciarra Poynyrt, t. (2010) *Louder Than Words: Take Your Career from Average to Exceptional with the Hidden Power of Nonverbal Intelligence*. Harper Collins Publishing.

[15] Howard, C. (2016) *Resilience: Your Super Power, A Practical Guide for High Performance Leadership*. Vibrant Radiant Health.

EQI 2.0 EMOTIONAL INTELLIGENCE ASSESSMENT

Would you like to have a baseline of the 16 dimensions of emotional intelligence?

We provide the leading assessment tool, EQi 2.0 20-page report, along with tools to help you get the most from this report:

- *Guide to Getting the Most from Your Report*
- A workbook to take you through each dimension to deepen your understanding and use of these skillsets.

Call 888-71-FOCUS

Cynthia Howard RN, CNC, PhD

C.A.R.E. METHOD™ AT YOUR ORGANIZATION

This is training in the four-step method to rewire your stress reaction and improve communication. It teaches the process and proven tools like mindfulness that will have lasting change on the level of stress people experience as well as the communication process.

This program is an excellent program for cross-functional teams involved in challenging change initiatives like lean sigma. It can be used as part of Conflict Competence training.

Contact Dr. Cynthia Howard and discuss how this program can be provided at your facility.

drh@eileadership.org

Care is the antidote to burnout— and the C.A.R.E. Method™ will help you care effectively.

Ei LEADERSHIP PROGRAMS

Ei Leadership provides executive and organizational development, consulting, and leadership training, utilizing Emotional Intelligence (Ei) tools and practices. We assess, coach, and train for strategic thinking using Ei, resilience strategies, and the Lean Six Sigma process.

Dr. Cynthia uses a variety of training options to provide the skills leaders need to be more effective and enjoy their work and home lives. Solving problems and making improvements is essential for work-life satisfaction.

Contact us today and schedule a complimentary session to find out which program is best for you and your work group.

Toll-free: 1-888-71-FOCUS

Coaching is the single greatest accelerator for change.

ABOUT THE AUTHOR

Pioneer of the resilient mindset. Cynthia has worked with scores of executives, healthcare professionals and organizations to transform complacency, conflict and turnover into consistent high performance.

Dr. Cynthia integrates the latest research in the fields of flow, resilience, emotional intelligence, and high performance within the structure of lean six sigma. This combination offers rapid, lasting change.

To contact Cynthia about this program, speaking at your organization, or for a consultation to use lean principles, call toll-free at 1-888-71-FOCUS or email drh@eileadership.org.

www.eileadership.org

OTHER BOOKS WRITTEN BY DR. CYNTHIA

**Resilience: Your Super Power
A Practical Guide for High Performance Leadership**

This is the foundation for the training program, The Resilient Leader System

www.resilientleaderprogram.com

Work S.M.A.R.T.: Stress Management and Resilience Training

Resources for an amazing career

www.worksmart.club

**HEAL: Healthy Emotions. Abundant Life.
From Superhero to Super Self-Empowered.
Master your Emotional Intelligence.**

Personal development

www.healprogram.com

Made in the USA
Columbia, SC
12 October 2017